Bodybuilders

HOLIDAY CLUB RESOURCE MATERIAL

PETER GRAYSTONE

•

A complete five-day holiday club programme for 5–11s

God centred and Bible based

Leaders' notes for preparation, teaching and activities

Serial drama scripts

Craft ideas

Activity sheets

All-age 'family service' outline

•

Scripture Union
130 City Road
London EC1V 2NJ

Thanks to ...

Bodybuilders was developed over two years at a Scripture Union event in Tockington, near Bristol in south-west England. Thanks to Celia, Paul, Pippa, Joel, Christian, Ben, Dan, Steve, Sarah, Jane, Moira, Rachel, Keith, Linda, Andy, Keith, Carol, Louise, Alan, Jackie, Helen, Esther, Debbie, Amanda, and Suzie. Special thanks to Angela Flynn for the title and original concept.

Please note: Publicity material designed especially for this programme is available from the Christian Publicity Organization, Garcia estate, Canterbury Road, Worthing, West Sussex, BN13 1BW.

© Peter Graystone 1993
First published 1993
Reprinted 1994

British Library Cataloguing in Publication Data
A catalogue record for this book is available from the British Library.

ISBN 0 86201 840 4

Cover by Julian Smith
Design and illustration by Tony Cantale Graphics

Printed in England by Ebenezer Baylis & Son Ltd, The Trinity Press, Worcester, and London.

Contents

Introduction

Bodybuilders is a five-day holiday club package for 5–11 year olds followed by a church service which is appropriate for all ages. It is suitable for use among children who have little or no knowledge of the Bible, but children who have Christian grown-ups at home will also find it thrilling. Alongside each other, both churched and unchurched children will increase their understanding of God's love for them, the uniqueness of Jesus, and his desire for them to follow him.

Bodybuilders moves at a lightning pace. It has moments of zaniness, but also quieter and more thoughtful stretches. Much of the programme takes place in small groups with children developing a relationship with particular leaders as they talk, make things, play and get messy together. The rest of the programme is a fast-moving presentation of truths from the Bible using music, teaching, drama and participation. The programme may be used on five consecutive mornings during school holidays or half-terms, but an alternative set of timings is given so that it may be adapted for use in term time, one evening per week for five weeks.

4

RUNNING
Bodybuilders

COUNTDOWN

10 months before the event – Make the decision to run a holiday club and confirm the dates with your own and other local church leaders. Book the hall where it will take place.

8 months before – Announce to the congregation that the holiday club will take place. Set in motion the means of financing it.

6 months before – Write to individuals in the church who have the potential to be presenters, group leaders, actors, musicians, aerobics instructors or refreshment makers. Invite them to join the team.

3 months before – Buy a copy of *Bodybuilders* for each member of the team. Try to identify what skills need to be developed in the team and plan how you can provide them with training in order to maximise the impact of the time they have with the children. Scripture Union's do-it-yourself training pack *Working with Children* may help you. (Price £18.34, including postage, from Scripture Union Training Unit, 26–30 Heathcoat Street, Nottingham, NG1 3AA.)

2 months before – Gather the leaders together to begin making detailed plans. Familiarize yourselves with the material, hold any training that has seemed desirable, make a list of the resources that are needed, allocate preparation tasks to particular people and pray together. Write to the Christian Publicity Organization, Garcia Estate, Canterbury Road, Worthing, West Sussex, BN13 1BW, to find out what publicity material is available.

1 month before – Remind the children of the church and their parents that *Bodybuilders* will take place. Invite them to book the dates and times in their diaries, if they haven't already done so.

2 weeks before – Advertise the event beyond the local congregation. Put up posters and distribute leaflets through front doors or in schools if permission is given. Take black and white photographs of half a dozen children trying out some of the zanier fun runs and send them to the news editor of the local paper with concise details of the event.

At least 1 week before – Meet with the leaders to pray and discuss any last minute requirements. Gather together all the resources that are needed. Do any photocopying that is required. Record the tannoy and ringing phone and check the aerobics music. Prepare the visual aids, including the five-part wall displays of bodies. Musicians and actors in the soap opera should have rehearsed and learnt their parts.

1 day before – Move into the hall, prepare the furniture and displays, set out as much equipment as possible. Only leave when the hall is ready to receive the first child.

1 hour before – Entire team arrives for Bible study and prayer.

Setting

The holiday club is set in 'Bodybuilders Health Club', an imaginary sports complex of a distinctly second-rate nature in a distinctly second-rate town. A soap opera runs from day to day, and the five characters in it are, supposedly, the five staff of the health club. In this setting the children take part in a physical workout (with aerobics, exercises and challenges) as well as a spiritual workout (with teaching, prayer and discussion). The programme glides from one to the other and back, so at times it is difficult to tell which category an activity belongs in. The 'health club' tannoy announces events, and also gives children information directly from the Bible.

The hall should be decorated to look like a gymnasium or sports club. At one end is a presentation and acting area. This area should be decorated with posters for sporting events. A large sign saying 'Bodybuilders Health Club' should be displayed, and pieces of gymnastic equipment (vaults or climbing bars, weights, exercise machines and so on) positioned to make a kind of stage set. Amongst these should be a desk with a telephone on it. Beside the acting area, a space is needed for the presenter of the event, an overhead projector and screen. And beside that, an area for the musicians! Children should be made aware that this end of the hall, which may contain a lot of expensive or even dangerous equipment, is for leaders only.

The rest of the hall is divided into two sections, the centre and the perimeter. The centre is a space (not with chairs, but perhaps with mats on the floor) in which children sit for the activities which are led from the front and involve everyone (warm up, aerobics, tannoy, team talk, lap of honour, action replay and shake out). Around the perimeter are areas marked out with circles of chairs (these will probably not be sat on, but they define a particular part of the hall as a 'base' for each child). Activities which take place in small groups happen in these areas (preview, fun run, work out and extra time). Beside each circle should be enough wall-space to build the life-size representation of a body which will grow limb by limb as the club progresses. Several times during each session children will move from the perimeter to the centre and back again. Symbols in the text show where each activity takes place.

GROUPS
Indicates an activity for which children are in groups

TOGETHER
Indicates an activity for which children are together

LEADERS
Indicates an activity for leaders only

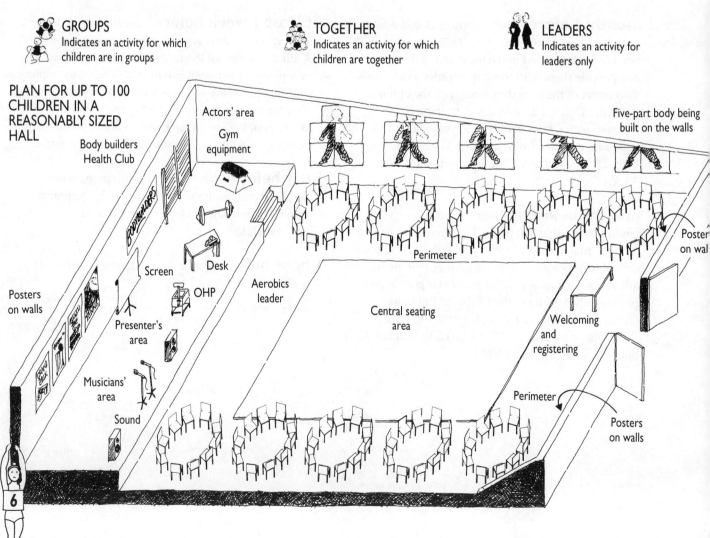

PLAN FOR UP TO 100 CHILDREN IN A REASONABLY SIZED HALL

Body builders Health Club

Actors' area

Gym equipment

Five-part body being built on the walls

Screen

Desk

Posters on walls

Presenter's area

OHP

Aerobics leader

Perimeter

Central seating area

Poster on wall

Welcoming and registering

Musicians' area

Sound

Perimeter

Posters on walls

Team

Groups

All the team should be encouraged to come as if dressed for sport. It is Scripture Union's urgent recommendation that there should be a ratio of at least one adult to every four children. They consist of the following people, although in some cases team members will play more than one role:

Vital
- Presenter; to host the event
- Speaker; to give short talks
- Actors; five of them
- Musicians
- Aerobics leader
- One leader for every small group of eight.
- At least two people to welcome and register children.

Desirable
- An extra leader for every small group
- Security; someone to patrol outside the hall
- Refreshment coordinator; for both children and team
- Hand-holders; to be available to take young children to the toilet, calm any who are in tears, fetch help in an emergency, and keep an eye on the team to see who needs encouragement, prayer or an extra pair of hands at any moment.

Luxury
- Extra 'cleaners up' and furniture arrangers
- Resource and technical equipment coordinator
- Rainy day standby

The most significant parts of *Bodybuilders* take place in small groups. Children are allocated to a particular group as soon as they arrive and stay with that group day by day. There are separate groups for 5–7 year olds and 8–11 year olds, and they have different activities at some points. Good friends should be kept together. An ideal number for each group is six to eight, but if at least two leaders are available for each group it may be possible to accommodate eleven or twelve.

The groups are named after parts of the body, and there should be a sign above each circle of chairs indicating the group's name. Some examples are given below. The chief function of the group leader is to befriend each child in his or her group. This is more important than any individual activity. During group events the leader should give instructions and encouragement, provide materials, organize each stage in the activity, and try to engage children in conversation. During up-front presentations, she or he should sit with the group on the floor. At the end of the club, each child should know his or her own group leader better than any other adult in the room and group leaders should know enough about the children in their care to be able to tell others the best way to pray about each one.

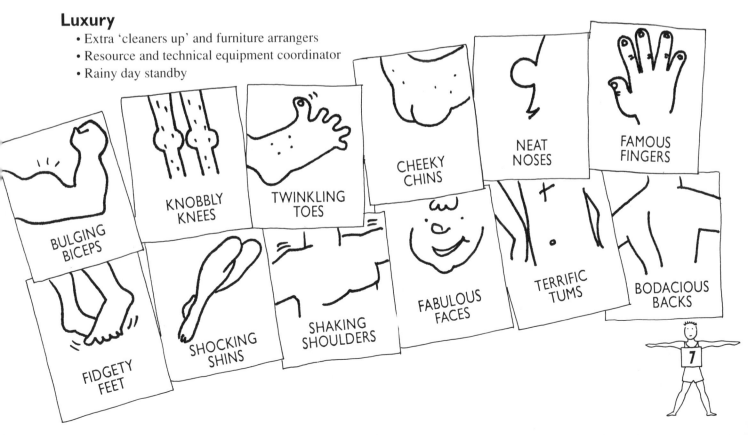

BULGING BICEPS

KNOBBLY KNEES

TWINKLING TOES

CHEEKY CHINS

NEAT NOSES

FAMOUS FINGERS

FIDGETY FEET

SHOCKING SHINS

SHAKING SHOULDERS

FABULOUS FACES

TERRIFIC TUMS

BODACIOUS BACKS

Body

During the course of the five sessions, each group builds a life-size body in two dimensions. The body is made out of five pieces of poster-sized card, and the outline of a body should be drawn faintly on the card in advance so that the picture can be kept in proportion from day to day. On each limb of the body, words or pictures are added by the groups as a record of the truths that have been discovered about God day by day. The body is built on the walls around the hall, attached with *Blu-Tack* or a similar adhesive.

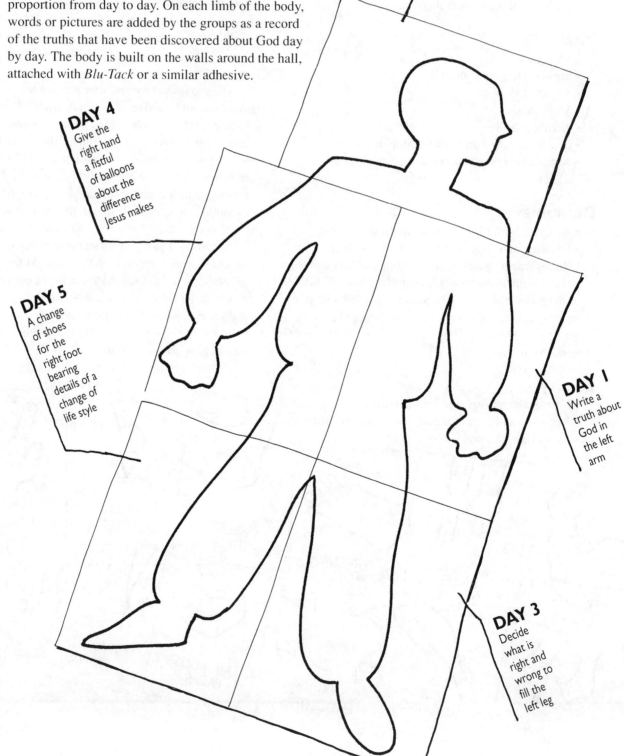

DAY 2
Surround the head with prayers in speech bubbles

DAY 4
Give the right hand a fistful of balloons about the difference Jesus makes

DAY 5
A change of shoes for the right foot bearing details of a change of life style

DAY 1
Write a truth about God in the left arm

DAY 3
Decide what is right and wrong to fill the left leg

The daily programmes

LEADERS' PREPARATION

Each day the leaders need to focus their minds on the task ahead before the children arrive. The programmes begin with suggestions for Bible study and prayer at an adult level. If the club is run in the morning, this should take up most of the time allocated, with only a few minutes given to last-minute preparations that cannot be done in advance. If the club takes place in the evening, this time is a shorter one with brief prayers, and a longer time of Bible study takes place after the children have left, in anticipation of the next day's subject.

PREVIEW

As children arrive they should be welcomed at the door. At least two people (more if there are large numbers of children) sit at a desk there. Their task is to record the name, telephone number and age of each child, and to decide which group to allocate children to. There are two categories of group, with names based on judo achievements – blue belts, for children aged 5–7; black belts, for children aged 8–11. Some flexibility is necessary here since it is important to keep good friends together, and brothers and sisters may have definite preferences for staying together or keeping apart! Since a large number of children need to be admitted in a short space of time, only a few details are needed at this stage and the record card on page 10 will give all the important information. If there is an emergency such as a fire, it is vital that the welcomers know who is in the room. If a child has an accident, the telephone number will be needed urgently, so it is important that it is recorded at the door while young children have an adult with them to

Timetables

Timings are given for both a morning and evening event.

9.30 or 6.15	Leaders arrive, prayer, last minute preparation
10.15 or 6.30	Children arrive, preview
10.30 or 6.45	Warm up
10.35 or 6.50	Fun run
10.40 or 6.55	Aerobics
10.44 or 6.59	Tannoy 1
10.45 or 7.00	Team talk
10.50 or 7.05	Work out
11.10 or 7.25	Tannoy 2
11.11 or 7.26	Lap of honour
11.20 or 7.35	Extra time
11.45 or 8.00	Action replay
11.55 or 8.10	Shake out
12.00 or 8.15	Crash out. Children leave. Leaders' evaluation, prayer, preparation
12.30 or 9.15	Leaders leave

Note that the children arrive from 10.15 but that the formal start is at 10.30, giving a ninety-minute programme. Work with under-eights lasting two hours or more must be registered with the local authority under The Children Act. Although there is no legal requirement to register a *Bodybuilders* club, you can only benefit by contacting the social services department for help and advice.

make sure it is correct. The same applies to special details, such as health or dietary requirements.

At this hectic time before the programme begins, anyone not leading a small group or registering children should be standing by the door, ready to take children to the group to which they have been allocated and introduce them by name to their group leader. While they are doing this, they must tell the children where the toilets are, where to hang their coats, and any other practical information.

REGISTRATION FORM

NAME

TELEPHONE

AGE

ATTENDANCE	DAY1	DAY2	DAY3	DAY4	DAY5

CATEGORY	BLUE BELT		BLACK BELT	

GROUP	BULGING BICEPS	FIDGETY FEET
	KNOBBLY KNEES	SHOCKING SHINS
	TWINKLING TOES	SHAKING SHOULDERS
	CHEEKY CHINS	FABULOUS FACES
	NEAT NOSES	TERRIFIC TUMS
	FAMOUS FINGERS	BODACIOUS BACKS

ANYTHING SPECIAL THE LEADERS SHOULD KNOW?

Tick the relevant boxes

Once the children have arrived at their small group, they are given either a blue belt or a black belt. This is a piece of material in the correct colour which they wear as a sash, like a judo or karate belt. During the course of the week, the children make large badges during this introductory session, and they pin the badges to the belt, so that progressively they gain more and more. The first time they come, they are given a badge on which the leader has written their name. They decorate it with felt-tipped pens and pin it to the bottom of the belt. In this way, every child can be actively involved as soon as he or she arrives.

While they are occupied with this, the leader should find out some information about them which is recorded on a separate and more detailed record card. This should be done in a friendly and relaxed way, so that children gain confidence in the leader. Obviously the groups will grow larger during this time as more children arrive.

RECORD CARD

NAME

AGE

GROUP

HOME ADDRESS

TELEPHONE NUMBER

PARENTS' NAME(S)

FRIEND WITH WHOM YOU CAME

HOW DID YOU HEAR ABOUT BODYBUILDERS?
(WHICH CHURCH, WHICH SCHOOL, WHICH FRIEND, ETC)

OTHER DETAILS (HEALTH ETC)?

WARM UP

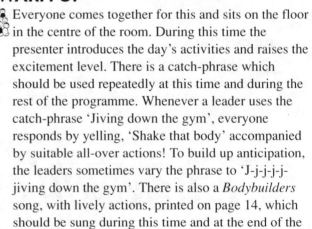

Everyone comes together for this and sits on the floor in the centre of the room. During this time the presenter introduces the day's activities and raises the excitement level. There is a catch-phrase which should be used repeatedly at this time and during the rest of the programme. Whenever a leader uses the catch-phrase 'Jiving down the gym', everyone responds by yelling, 'Shake that body' accompanied by suitable all-over actions! To build up anticipation, the leaders sometimes vary the phrase to 'J-j-j-j-j-jiving down the gym'. There is also a *Bodybuilders* song, with lively actions, printed on page 14, which should be sung during this time and at the end of the session.

FUN RUN

This is an entirely frivolous, usually messy activity. It is introduced by the presenter, but children go to their small groups to try it out.

AEROBICS

Led by an enthusiastic and energetic leader, these exercises should take place in the centre of the room to the accompaniment of a loud disco track with a clear rhythm. The music should be up-to-date and familiar to children from the mainstream pop chart, but check the suitability of the words! The movements should be simple, repetitive and not likely to strain muscles! If in doubt, borrow a beginners' tape from a video library, remembering that children are not capable of so rigorous a routine as adults! It is important that a tape deck with a sufficiently powerful amplification to fill the hall is used.

TANNOY 1

At the height of the aerobics, a disembodied voice should interrupt the music with no warning at all. It tells the children what to do (sit down and listen) and then gives them a reading taken directly from the Good News Bible. The voice should be a deep, authoritative one which has been pre-recorded on to a tape. The simplest way to do this is to use a twin-deck cassette player which will switch from the music to the previously cued-up voice at the press of a button. This will take children by surprise on the first day (although they will come to expect it), so leaders should show them what to do by example, not instruction. A full script for the tannoy is given on page 57.

TEAM TALK

The speaker should give this short talk, not exceeding four minutes. Although the notes for each day give a script for the talk, it should not under any circumstances be read. The speaker should not feel constrained, either, to adhere rigidly to this suggested talk. Examples and anecdotes from personal experience are far more effective than any published wording. The script given, though, should help the speaker pitch correctly the tone, level, length and visual content of the talk. From it, notes can be made and overhead projector transparencies produced.

WORK OUT

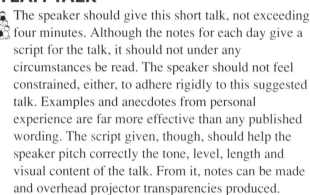

The speaker should conclude his talk by sending children to their small groups. The group leaders give instructions for the activity, which always begins with drawing, colouring and adding details to the part of the body which is being added to the wall-display that day. At this point, groups of 5–7 year olds have different, less complex activities from groups of 8–11 year olds. Two minutes before the end of the activity, the presenter should go to each group in turn and warn the leader that he or she should be coming to the end. This is because the instructions for the next event will come abruptly.

TANNOY 2

This tannoy message cuts in to the previous activity with the same unexpected authority as the first one. The pause between the instruction and the message should be longer to give children time to come to the centre of the room and sit down. Whoever is operating the cassette button must make sure that the children are in place before the Bible extract is heard.

LAP OF HONOUR

This is a lively and joyful time of praise to God, interspersed with prayers. The musicians should teach songs carefully, assuming that they will be unknown to the children, who may never have been to church before. Include the *Bodybuilders* song, and repeat the same few songs again and again, so that they become familiar. Action songs are particularly appropriate to the week's theme. When it comes to prayers, it should be explained to whom we are speaking and why. The suggested prayers grow in complexity and involvement as days go by. Written permission must be obtained from the publishers of songs whose words are displayed on an overhead projector.

EXTRA TIME

At this point, the organisers of the holiday club have a choice.

If the club has been aiming to make contact with children who never go to church, there has already been precisely the right amount of Bible teaching content in the programme. During this session, the children should go to their groups for a relaxed craft activity. An extensive list of ideas is given on pages 63 and 64. While this is taking place, the leaders should be looking for opportunities to engage children in conversation and get to know them by sharing information about their families, likes and dislikes, favourite music and television, and so on. It may be that a child asks a question about God, the club or the church. The leader should answer this in a friendly way, inviting the opinions of other members of the group, as they continue to work at the craft. If the leader is able to explain why he or she is a Christian, this can be a very valuable experience for a child. However, these opportunities should not under any circumstances be forced by a leader – pray instead that the Holy Spirit will prompt these subjects to arise in conversation in his time and in his way.

If the club has been organized primarily for the children with whom the church is already in touch, it may be appropriate to spend this time reading a Bible story. If this option is chosen, each small group needs a photocopy of the appropriate poster for the day – these appear at the end of each day's programme. The poster should be placed on the floor with the children sitting or sprawling around it. The leader should follow the instructions through three stages – firstly, a series of simple exercises; secondly, a Bible passage which is printed on the poster and some questions to help children discuss it; thirdly, a way of praying as a group. When the poster is complete, it should be displayed on the wall alongside the body, one being added each day.

In reality, the children who attend the holiday club will not fall exclusively into a single category –

church or unchurched. A careful decision needs to be taken about which stream to choose so that the majority of the children are stretched, but not so overdosed with Bible material that they become confused. The presenters should again give leaders two minutes' warning of the end of the activity, but this time it is not interrupted by a tannoy (which would be a most unfortunate interruption to a time of prayer). Instead, leaders should bring their groups to sit in the centre of the hall.

ACTION REPLAY

 A soap opera for five actors! The scripts reflect each day's theme, but only in an understated way. The overall impact of the drama may help the children anticipate the help the Holy Spirit will give them as they seek to follow Jesus.

SHAKE OUT

 After the drama, a reprise of the *Bodybuilders* song may be desirable. Notices should be given at this point (perhaps booming over the tannoy again). Each day a quick group-building activity is suggested as a means of saying goodbye. Close the session with a reminder that next day (or week) the children should again come jiving down the gym. 'Shake that body!'

CRASH OUT

 Children leave at this point. Since the leaders are responsible for the children's welfare, make sure that they are leaving with the correct adult, and that no one leaves unaccompanied or with someone whom they were not expecting would collect them unless you are satisfied that this is their parent's intention. If adults have arrived early, invite them to watch the last few minutes of the programme standing at the back of the hall.

When all the children have gone, the leaders should interrupt the clearing up. They should sit down together and reflect on the day's programme. What worked well and what could be improved? Did the children discover what you hoped they would and what modifications to the programme are needed? What children need specific prayers and for what can you give thanks to God? Follow this with a time of prayer. If the club is in the evening, look ahead to the teaching of the next day (or week) and study the Bible passage. Go on to talk about what practical preparations are required for the next session. Then finish clearing up and get the hall as ready as possible for the next session, freeing yourselves to spend the minutes before the children arrive in prayer rather than in panic!

After Bodybuilders

Immediately after the event, details of children's names and addresses should be collated so that personal invitations can be sent to any events which follow up the holiday club.

PERSONAL CONTACT

Most children enjoy receiving letters. Group leaders could be encouraged to write to those for whom they have been responsible, referring back to their shared experience of *Bodybuilders*. Such letters should be kept low key and comments about the way a particular child developed spiritually during the week should not be made in a way which parents would find threatening or mysterious. Any invitation to meet the child again should be completely above suspicion, which probably means that the invitation should be extended to the parents as well.

MIDWEEK CLUBS

An after-school or early-evening club may prove popular. It should contain a *Bodybuilders* style mix of games, craft and Christian input. Scripture Union's Sound and Vision unit produce a range of videos and accompanying activity material which are suitable for children without a great deal of experience or knowledge of Christianity. Write for a catalogue to: Sound and Vision Unit, Scripture Union, 130 City Road, London EC1V 2NJ. Mention that your church has been following the *Bodybuilders* programme.

FAMILY EVENTS

By sending children to a holiday club, some parents who have had no other connection with a church become a kind of 'fringe' to the congregation through this first involvement. A non-threatening recreational event for all ages together would bring them into contact with Christian people in a more relaxed way than a church service. This could be a barn dance, a barbecue, a sports day, a firework party, a treasure hunt or an outing. It should be an active time (not, for example, a film show during which no one talks to anyone else) and the Christian content should be tiny, but of good quality (a well-constructed prayer of thanks before a meal is of far more value than a 'you've-had-the-candy-now-here's-the-medicine' epilogue)! With God's grace and the friendship of

Christians the 'fringe' of a church becomes, in time, the congregation of a church – and creates its own new fringe!

SUNDAY PROGRAMME

Children who have enjoyed a regular midweek club may grow in their understanding of Christian basics to such an extent that a weekly Sunday morning programme is suitable for them. Scripture Union's 'SALT' programme, available from Autumn 1993, offers a structured programme of Bible teaching, application to life, praise and prayer. Whilst not as formal as a traditional Sunday School, its interactive package of stories, discussions, games and craft provides foundation teaching and worship for children of all ages, and a parallel programme for adults and 'family' services. Details of the scheme can be obtained from: Publishing department, Scripture Union, 130 City Road, London EC1V 2NJ. Specify whether you are interested in:

SALT: 3 to 4 plus, with its integrated activity package, *Sparklers.*

SALT: 5 to 7 plus with its integrated activity package, *Allstars.*

SALT: 8 to 10 plus, with its integrated activity package, *Trailblazers.*

SALT: 11 to 13 plus, with its integrated activity package, *LAZER.*

SALT: all ages – for adult sermons and all-age 'family' service resources.

Other resources

All are published by Scripture Union unless otherwise stated.

Splash! – activities for under 5s

Springboard – activities for 7–11s

Launchpad – activities for 11–14s

You're Only Young Once! – YOYO! four volumes of activities for teenage youth clubs

Help! There's a Child in my Church! – Peter Graystone's book of advice on working with 7–11s

Reaching Children – Paul Butler's book on children's evangelism

Family Evangelism – John Hattam (published by and available from the Scripture Union Missions Department)

Find Out – six volumes of Bible reading activities for 5–7s to use with parents

Quest – a quarterly Bible reading scheme for 7–11s

One to One – a quarterly Bible reading scheme for 10–13s

Praise God Together, Let's Join In, Junior Praise (Marshall Pickering) – song books in which most of the listed songs can be found

THE BODYBUILDERS LOGO

The logo may be used to raise the profile of the holiday club – on publicity material, T-shirts, badges and so on. Within the club, too, use it to give children a sense of belonging. Further publicity material, designed especially for this programme, is available from the Christian Publicity Organization, Garcia Estate, Canterbury Road, Worthing, West Sussex BN13 1BW.

The Bodybuilders song

Words Peter Graystone Music Derek Llewellyn
Dance movements by Paul Sharpe

Every action slightly anticipates the word it accompanies

Bodybuilders, bodybuilders Getting into shape to fol-low Je-sus

Bodybuilders, bodybuilders Working out how we can fol-low him

Exer–cising, real-izing Jesus loves us so much it's sur-pri-sing

Jive! (Shake your body) Jive! (Shake your body)

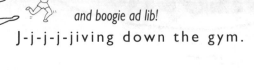

and boogie ad lib!

J-j-j-j-jiving down the gym.

DAY I

Left arm day

GOD MADE ME AND I AM PRECIOUS
Psalm 139:1–24, John 2:1–12

3.30 6.15

LEADERS' PREPARATION

Pray that every leader will come to appreciate their specialness to God, and will realize and fulfil the unique purpose God has for them on the team.

Read Psalm 139:1–24 and John 2:1–12, then discuss some or all of these questions:

1 Psalm 139 helps us realise that God sees and understands everything about us. Is it good news or bad news for us that nothing is hidden from him? Do verses 5 and 24 suggest that it is a comfort or a challenge?

2 What kinds of thing does God know about the children who will take part in *Bodybuilders*, which you do not know?

3 Verses 19–22 of Psalm 139 talk about opposition to God's work. Do you sense opposition to the work you are doing for him? How do you react to the strength or feeling shown by the writer here?

4 Read John 2:1–12. What do you think Mary was expecting when she spoke to Jesus in verse 3? What did she learn about Jesus from this incident?

Invite everyone in the group to share one thing they are looking forward to and one thing which they are anxious about with regard to *Bodybuilders*. Pray together about what you have heard.

(If the club takes place in the evening, use only the final prayers at this point – the Bible study having taken place on a previous occasion. [See page 9]. Continue to adapt the preparation in this way day by day.)

10.15 6.30

PREVIEW

Welcome and register children, then lead them to their small groups in the way described on page 9. Give each one the correct coloured belt and his or her first badge, made from card and a safety pin. Today, the child's name should be written on the badge, and felt-tipped pens should be provided for children to decorate and illuminate the name as imaginatively as possible. Group leaders use this time to talk to and take records of each individual child. They can also be given a *Bodybuilders* logo badge to colour and begin to build up their collection on the belt.

10.30 6.45

WARM UP

The presenter introduces the event, establishes the catch-phrase and response, teaches the *Bodybuilders* song and actions.

10.35 6.50

FUN RUN

Today's activity is a beauty contest. Each group should select one member (if necessary, the leader). They have three minutes to make him or her as striking as possible using make-up, hair gel, a new hairstyle and so on. Line up the models or allow them to parade as if on a catwalk. Encourage lots of cheering and applause, and congratulate both serious attempts and grotesquery. Boys will enjoy this every bit as much as girls!

10.40 6.55

AEROBICS

Simple and fast–moving exercises to music, interrupted by the unexpected....

10.44 6.59

TANNOY I

God made my whole being. He formed me in my mother's body. I praise him because he made me in an amazing and wonderful way. What you have done is wonderful. All the days planned for me were written in your book before I was one day old. (From Psalm 139:13–16)

AT THE TOP OF A MOUNTAIN IN NEPAL...

TEAM TALK

Many many miles away, in one of the world's far-flung corners, there is a small kingdom called Nepal. It is one of the most beautiful countries in the world. Its snow-capped mountains stretch upward so wild and so remote that many of them have never been climbed by a human being. The top of the very furthest one is a land of snow and ice – so cold, so rugged that barely any wildlife can survive. And in the very highest peak of that icy world is a deep cave, never glimpsed by a living soul, choked by glaciers and cluttered with boulders. And in the deepest corner of that terrifying cave is a hollow. And at the furthest end of that icy hollow is a pebble. And underneath that tiny pebble are some grains of sand. Someone I know has counted exactly how may grains of sand are there!

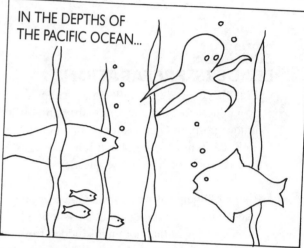

IN THE DEPTHS OF THE PACIFIC OCEAN...

Across the other side of the world is the largest expanse of water on earth, the Pacific Ocean. It teems with living creatures – whales, sharks and sting-rays. In the deepest vault of that purple ocean is a ravine that plunges down into unfathomable blackness. That ravine contains a dark cave, never glimpsed by a living soul. And in that awesome cave swim creatures, so strange and mysterious that you would gasp to see them, with shapes that there is no word for and no hint of a colour that the eye could detect. And every year those marine creatures reproduce in their hundreds and thousands to make the seas teem with good things. Someone I know has a name for every newborn creature there.

Who is it that knows these unknowable things? His name is God. You may have heard of him, for people use his name all day long – sometimes when they are thankful or in need, or sometimes when they are angry or bored or feel like swearing (which must really upset him).

GOD KNOWS EVERY DETAIL OF YOUR FINGERPRINT

HE LOVES EVERYTHING ABOUT YOU

It is God who made this world and everything in it. He made it out of nothing at the beginning of time. And now he keeps it going, day by day, hour by hour, second by second. He is so astronomically big and so sensationally powerful that he knows all there is to know about his world.

And (this will astonish you).... he knows all there is to know about you. He knows every detail of your fingerprint; he knows how many hairs are on your head; he knows what make of trainers you wear; he knows what you dream about at night; he knows what makes you leap for joy; he knows what makes you cry, even when you don't want to tell anyone else. He knows this because fingerprints and hair and trainers and dreams and happiness and tears were all God's idea in the first place.

I am about to tell you the most important thing I

16

know! And I think it is the most important thing you will ever find out in your whole life. That makes today a very special day, so listen carefully because here it comes ... God loves you!

He loves everything about you! He likes everything about you! Even if you have no one else in the world who loves you, you are not alone, because God loves you. Even if you feel left out because of your shape or your voice or the colour of your skin, you are not alone, because God loves you. Even if you feel you are not good enough, or not friendly enough, or not clever enough, you are not alone, because God loves you.

He always has! He does at this moment! He always will!

10.50 / 7.05
WORK OUT

 Each group should collect its poster of a left arm (see page 8), go over the faintly traced outline with a felt marker, then work together to colour it in, add clothes, jewellery, details and so on. Attach it to the wall.

5–7s: Make a large picture headed 'Everyone is special to God' by cutting photographs of people and particularly faces from magazines, then pasting them together as a montage. As this is done, the leader should talk with the children about what makes each person in the picture unique – a special skin colour, a special hair colour, a special shape or size, and so on. When the picture is completed, put it on the wall so that it looks as if the hand is holding it up.

8–11s: Split the group into pairs and give each pair one of the six cards cut from page 22. Invite them to solve the codes: A=1, B=2, C=3 and so on. (The solutions are: God really loves me, I am precious to God, God knows all about me, God thinks humans are great, God cares for me totally, I was created by God.) When all have finished, each pair should report what their code has revealed (some pairs may have two, or cards may be left out, depending on size or speed). After considering them, a group decision should be reached as to which is the most wonderful of the truths. This can be achieved by consensus, discussion, vote or lottery! The leader should write the selected phrase inside or next to the left arm on the poster. There may be time to look at other groups' work before the unexpected....

11.10 / 7.25
TANNOY 2

Lord, you know all about me. You know when I sit down and when I get up. You know my thoughts before I think them. Even before I say a word, you already know what I am going to say. You are all around me – in front and at the back. You have put your hand on me. (From Psalm 139:1–5)

11.11 / 7.26
LAP OF HONOUR

A lively time of praise to God, focusing on his greatness and his care. Particularly appropriate songs are: 'Have you seen the pussycat?', 'Father God, I

wonder how I managed to exist', 'My God is so great (big)' or 'God is good'. The *Bodybuilders* song could also be sung. At some point during the singing, use this chant as a prayer, the leader saying the alternative lines rhythmically and everyone responding with the repeated italic phrase:

God has filled the earth with beauty,
All the world give God your praises,
Worship is your joy and duty,
All the world give God your praises,
Who filled up the sea with water?
All the world give God your praises,
Made each child a son or daughter?
All the world give God your praises,
Made cows moo and set snakes hissing?
All the world give God your praises,
Who invented hugs and kissing?
All the world give God your praises,
Who decided stars would twinkle?
All the world give God your praises,
Eyes would wink and foreheads wrinkle?
All the world give God your praises,
Whose idea were films and telly?
All the world give God your praises,
Who makes Stilton cheese so smelly?
All the world give God your praises,
Only God could be that clever,
All the world give God your praises,
Let his praises sound forever,
All the world give God your praises.

11.20 / 7.35
EXTRA TIME

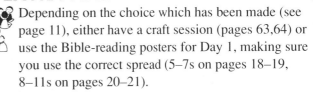 Depending on the choice which has been made (see page 11), either have a craft session (pages 63,64) or use the Bible-reading posters for Day 1, making sure you use the correct spread (5–7s on pages 18–19, 8–11s on pages 20–21).

11.45 / 8.00
ACTION REPLAY

The script for part 1 of the soap opera is on page 58.

11.55 / 8.10
SHAKE OUT

 The presenter should give out announcements which need to be made. Then, as a way of saying goodbye, challenge everyone to shake hands with as many people in the room as they possibly can in sixty seconds. Remind them to give their belts to their group leaders before they leave. Close by inviting everyone to spend tomorrow jiving down the gym! Shake that body!

1 Tone up

Crouch down on the floor, then jump as high as you can stretching your arms and legs out. 5 times. Then sit down in a circle round the chart.

2 All quiet

Your leader will read you a story about Jesus. He is God's own Son. The story about him comes from the Bible. Listen, while you look at the pictures.

18

3 Muscle builder

Two days later there was a wedding in the town of Cana in Galilee. Jesus' mother was there, and Jesus and his disciples had also been invited to the wedding. When the wine had given out, Jesus' mother said to him, "They have no wine left."

"You must not tell me what to do," Jesus replied. "My time has not yet come."

Jesus' mother then told the servants, "Do whatever he tells you."

The Jews have rules about ritual washing, and for this purpose six stone water jars were there, each one large enough to hold about a hundred litres. Jesus said to the servants, "Fill these jars with water." They filled them to the brim, and then he told them, "Now draw some water out and take it to the man in charge of the feast."

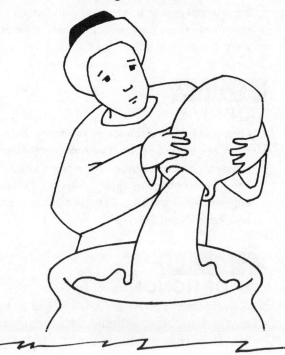

They took him the water, which now had turned into wine, and he tasted it. He did not know where this wine had come from (but, of course, the servants who had drawn out the water knew); so he called the bridegroom and said to him, "Everyone else serves the best wine first, and after the guests have had plenty to drink, he serves the ordinary wine. But you have kept the best wine until now!"

Jesus performed this first miracle in Cana in Galilee; there he revealed his glory, and his disciples believed in him. After this, Jesus and his mother, brothers, and disciples went to Capernaum and stayed there a few days.

4 Body stretch

How amazing Jesus was to be able to turn water into wine! Has anyone in the group heard of Jesus before? If so, they can tell everyone else what they know about Jesus.

Jesus loved going to parties. If he came to your party, what would you give him to eat and drink? Everyone can draw their idea in the space while the rest of the group guess what they have drawn.

Anyone who wants to can say a prayer thanking God for the lovely foods you have drawn. Your leader will explain how to do this.

19

DAY 1
Black belts

1 Tone up

Crouch down as low as possible and jump up into a
star shape. 6 times. Stand up. Lift your right knee to
touch your left elbow, then your left knee to touch
your right elbow. 10 times. Then sit down in a circle
round the chart.

2 All quiet

This is the first of a series of posters about Jesus.
Christians believe he is the Son of God. This story
about him comes from the Bible. Your leader will say
a prayer that you understand what this story can teach
us. Then someone can read it out.

Jesus went to lots of parties. If he came to your party,
what would you give him to eat and what kind of
activities do you think he'd like to join in? Write your
answers here.

This means people who
followed Jesus because they
wanted to learn from him.

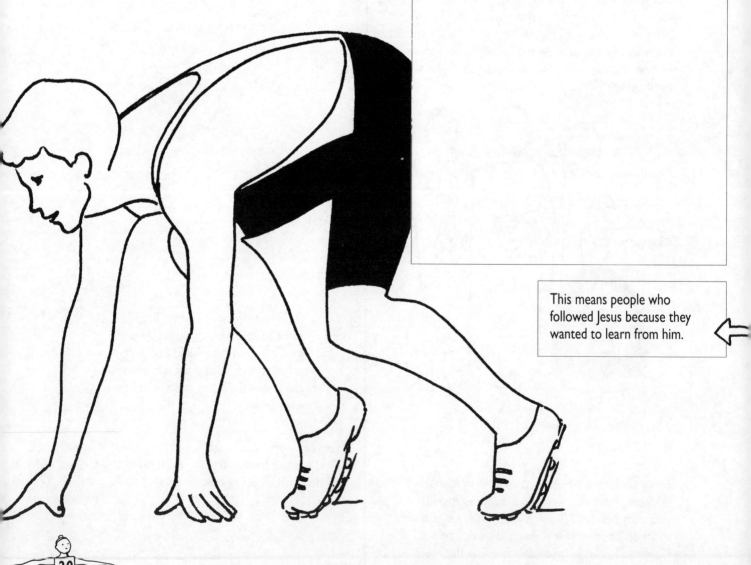

20

3 Muscle builder

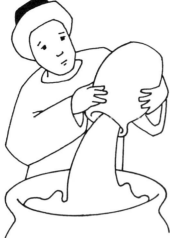

Two days later there was a wedding in the town of Cana in Galilee. Jesus' mother was there, and Jesus and his disciples had also been invited to the wedding. When the wine had given out, Jesus' mother said to him, "They have no wine left."

"You must not tell me what to do," Jesus replied. "My time has not yet come."

Jesus' mother then told the servants, "Do whatever he tells you."

The Jews have rules about ritual washing, and for this purpose six stone water jars were there, each one large enough to hold about a hundred litres.

Jesus said to the servants, "Fill these jars with water." They filled them to the brim, and then he told them, "Now draw some water out and take it to the man in charge of the feast." They took him the water, which now had turned into wine, and he tasted it. He did not know where this wine had come from (but, of course, the servants who had drawn out the water knew); so he called the bridegroom and said to him, "Everyone else serves the best wine first, and after the guests have had plenty to drink, he serves the ordinary wine. But you have kept the best wine until now!"

Jesus performed this first miracle in Cana in Galilee; there he revealed his glory, and his disciples believed in him. After this, Jesus and his mother, brothers, and disciples went to Capernaum and stayed there a few days.

John 2:1–12

What do you think Mary said to her friends when she saw what happened?

4 Body stretch

Think of some words which this story makes you feel about Jesus. Everyone who wants to can tell Jesus what they feel. You put the word you thought of in this sentence:

Lord Jesus, you are . . . . Amen.

One at a time, say it to him. Then your leader will say a prayer that you will really enjoy this holiday club.

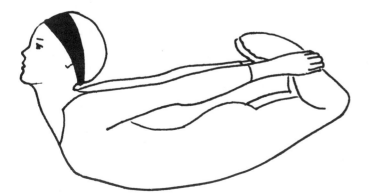

CRASH OUT

After the children have left, the leaders should gather together before they lose their momentum. Begin by thanking God for what has happened on the first day, regardless of what problems have arisen. Then share reactions to the day's events and pray about the programme for the next day. (If the club is being held in the evening, study the next day's Bible passages.) Prepare the room for Day 2 as much as possible before leaving.

YOU WILL NEED:

At the door:
- Registration forms
- Pen

Presenter's area:
- Overhead projector
- Acetates: words of songs, prayer and illustration for talk
- Sound system
- Cassette player, cassettes of tannoy messages, aerobics music, and phone ringing
- Soap opera properties

In groups:
- Blue or black belts
- Badges; or card, scissors, *Sellotape*, safety pins
- Detailed forms
- Felt-tipped pens
- Odds and ends of make-up, hair gel, combs, brushes – collected from members of the congregation who have finished with, regretted buying, or received them as unwanted gifts!
- Left arm poster, felt marker, *Blu-Tack*, card, magazines, scissors, paste (5–7s), code cards, pencils (8–11s)
- Craft equipment or Bible-reading posters.

See WORK OUT 8–11s on page 17

DAY 2

Head day

I CAN PRAY TO GOD AND HE RESPONDS
Matthew 6:5–15; Mark 1:35–45

9.30 / 6.15

LEADERS' PREPARATION

Thank God that he is a God who listens, understands and responds, no matter what the circumstances in which we pray to him.

Read Matthew 6:5–15 and Mark 1:35–45, then discuss some or all of these questions:

1 If God knows what we need when we pray about *Bodybuilders* (Matthew 6:8), why bother?

2 Jesus is very critical of some people's prayers here. Where in this age would one come across mindless, meaningless prayers? Having identified them, can you see any value at all in them?

3 What difference should these instructions of Jesus make to the way we pray about *Bodybuilders*?

4 Read Mark 1:35–45. What can this teach us about the way we treat children we like instantly and those who are hard to like? How can we make sure we approach them with the same attitude as Jesus?

Pray for the day's activities in the way which seems most appropriate after the discussion – silently, in pairs, as a group, led by one person, or whatever.

10.15 / 6.30

PREVIEW

Welcome and register children, then lead them to their groups. On today's badge, children should draw and colour all the people who live at home with them, including their pets. If children are making their own badges as well as drawing them, they could be made in the shape of their home (house, flat, terrace, bungalow, etc).

10.30 / 6.45

WARM UP

Sing the *Bodybuilders* song, use the catch-phrase, and so on.

10.35 / 6.50

FUN RUN

Put the group into pairs. Everyone should take off their shoes and spread them across the space. Place a flat chocolate-covered mint such as an 'After Eight' mint between the two foreheads of the pair. They are to collect their shoes and put them on without dropping the 'After Eight' mint. If they succeed they may eat what little is left of it!

10.40 / 6.55
AEROBICS

Simple exercises with only slight variations on the previous day's routine.

10.44 / 6.59

TANNOY 1

The Lord is pleased with an honest person's prayer. If one of you is having troubles, he should pray. If one is happy he should sing praises. When a good person prays, great things happen. (From Proverbs 15:8; James 5:13–16)

10.45 / 7.00

TEAM TALK

Do you remember that yesterday we talked about God, who made the world and loves us? Well, all those who are on the '*Bodybuilders*' team live their lives with God as their friend and try to please him in what they do. Sometimes they call God 'the Lord', as the voice on the tannoy did – it is a way of saying how important he is.

Can we see God? No! He is invisible – and anyway he is so big and so powerful that it would be too much for the human eye to manage. However, we can talk to God. In fact yesterday, after you had gone home, all the leaders sat down together and told God what was on their minds. We thanked him for the

23

good things which happened yesterday; we asked that today would be enjoyable; and we told him all about you and how we wanted you to have a good time. This is called praying. Praying is usually enjoyable to do. God wants everyone to do it (just like your friends want you to talk to them), and he always, always listens. You can pray with your eyes shut or open; God listens. You can write your prayer down, or speak it, or just think it; God listens. You can pray together with other people or by yourself; God listens. What a marvellous God we have!

Before some of you were born, or perhaps when you were still very young, there was a man who lived in England called Terry Waite. He was a determined friend of God, and part of his job was to persuade those who kept people prisoner for wrong reasons to release them. One day he went to Lebanon, which is a beautiful country that had been tragically damaged by war and fighting, in order to persuade a violent group of fighters to release some hostages they had taken prisoner. To everyone's dismay, he was taken prisoner himself. All over the world, people who regard God as a friend started to pray for Terry to be set free. They prayed on and on for about five years, even when it was not certain whether Terry was still alive. Sometimes it seemed as if God was not listening, because nothing happened. Then, on a remarkable day in December 1991, Terry Waite was set free. Those who had been praying were sure that God had heard their prayer and done what they asked, even though they had waited a very, very long time. And then, of course, they said thank you to God over and over and over again.

You can pray to God too. He will always listen. When you say thank you to him for things you like about the world he made, he will be delighted. When you ask him for things you need, he will listen. Of course, he will never give us things which are bad for us – that would be like playing a trick on us, like giving us a stone when we asked for a sandwich! So sometimes when we ask for things, God gives us something different from what we ask for – but it will always be better for us, even if it doesn't seem so at the time. So we can pray confidently knowing that, whatever happens, God is being good and loving to us.

Pray in good times! Pray in bad times! Pray and watch out to see what God will do!

YOU CAN PRAY....

TERRY WAITE

A STONE INSTEAD OF A SANDWICH

`10.50` `7.05`
WORK OUT

Colour and add detail to the poster of a head and place it above the left arm.

5–7s: Talk with the children about the things they most enjoy about life – prompt them to suggest, perhaps, their favourite foods, games, animals, television programmes. Give each of them a large speech bubble drawn on coloured paper. Remind the children that it is only because of God's goodness to the world he made that we have these things to enjoy. Invite them to choose some things they would like to thank God for and to draw them in the speech bubble. When they have done this, they should cut them out and display them all round the head.

8–11s: Invite the group to form pairs and give each pair a speech bubble drawn on coloured paper. Suggest that they talk to their partner about what they would particularly like to say to God in prayer, either thanking him for or asking for something. (The leader may need to suggest ideas.) They should write their prayer in the speech bubble, or draw it if they prefer, since God will understand just as well. It should be cut out and arranged on the wall beside the head.

`11.10` `7.25`
TANNOY 2

Always be happy. Never stop praying. Give thanks whatever happens. That is what God wants for you in Christ Jesus. (From 1 Thessalonians 5:16–18)

`11.11` `7.26`
LAP OF HONOUR

Songs of praise to God which largely repeat those learnt on Day 1, with perhaps one new song which relates to today's subject. Suitable songs would be 'Talk to God and share with him' or 'Thank you Lord God for this fine day'. At some point during the singing, focus on the prayers children have written or drawn. While the workout was in progress, the presenter should have observed what is going on in the groups and chosen four or five of the prayers, representing a cross section of moving ones, barely coherent ones and drawn ones. He or she should either read them aloud, asking everyone to share in the prayer to God, or invite the children who wrote them to read them, or put into words what has been drawn. Permission should, of course, be requested politely from the children who created the prayers.

`11.20` `7.35`
EXTRA TIME

Either craft activities or Bible-reading posters (5–7s on pages 26–27, 8–11s on pages 28–29).

`11.45` `8.00`
ACTION REPLAY

The script for part 2 of the soap opera is on page 59.

`11.55` `8.10`
SHAKE OUT

Give announcements, use the catch-phrase, and say goodbye by challenging everyone to shake feet with as many people as possible in sixty seconds.

`12.00` `8.15`
CRASH OUT

After the children have left, gather the leaders and ask them to share with the rest of the group something about one child who has caught their attention over the past two days – either because of a particular need or a special joy. Spend time praying for these children in particular before commenting on and thanking God for the rest of the day's activities. Prepare for Day 3.

YOU WILL NEED:

At the door:
- Registration forms
- Pen

Presenter's area:
- Overhead projector
- Acetates: words of songs and illustrations
- Sound system
- Cassette player, cassettes of tannoy messages, aerobics music and phone ringing
- Soap opera properties

In groups:
- Blue or black belts
- Badges, or card, scissors, *Sellotape*, safety pins
- Detailed forms
- Felt-tipped pens
- After Eight or similar chocolate mints
- Head poster, felt marker, *Blu–Tack*
- Coloured paper with speech bubbles or photocopies
- Craft equipment or Bible-reading posters

DAY 2
Blue belts

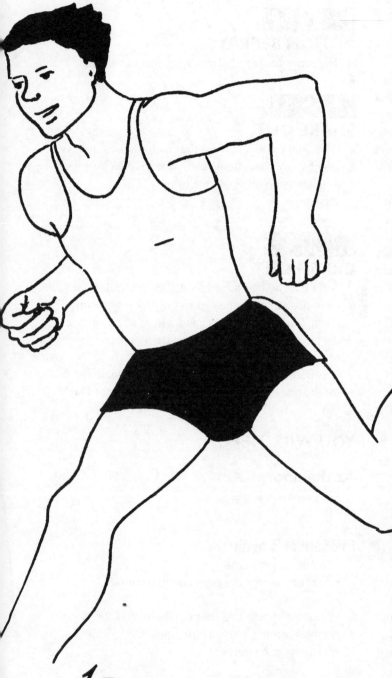

3 Muscle builder

A man suffering from a dreaded skin-disease came to Jesus, knelt down, and begged him for help. "If you want to," he said, "you can make me clean."

Jesus was filled with pity, and stretched out his hand and touched him. "I do want to," he answered. "Be clean!"

1 Tone up

Clap your hands above your head, then bend your knees and touch the ground. 10 times. Then sit down in a circle round the chart.

2 All quiet

Your leader will say a prayer asking God to help you understand this part of the Bible. Then listen to today's story.

4 Body stretch

Sick people are sometimes still healed today when Christians pray for them. If it is God's plan for them to be well again, he will work alongside doctors to heal them. Ask your leader if he or she has known this to happen. Then anyone in the group can talk about a time when they were ill and how they got better.

If you know some people who are ill, tell your leader their names, and he or she will write them on the hand.

At once the disease left the man, and he was clean. Then Jesus spoke sternly to him and sent him away at once, after saying to him, "Listen, don't tell anyone about this. But go straight to the priest and let him examine you; then in order to prove to everyone that you are cured, offer the sacrifice that Moses ordered."

But the man went away and began to spread the news everywhere. Indeed, he talked so much that Jesus could not go into a town publicly. Instead, he stayed out in lonely places, and people came to him from everywhere.

Say some prayers asking God to heal the people whose names are written on the hand. Your leader will explain how to do this.

27

DAY 2
Black belts

3 Muscle builder

A man suffering from a dreaded skin-disease came to Jesus, knelt down, and begged him for help. "If you want to," he said, "you can make me clean."

Jesus was filled with pity, and stretched out his hand and touched him. "I do want to." he answered. "Be clean!" At once the disease left the man, and he was clean. Then Jesus spoke sternly to him and sent him away at once, after saying to him, "Listen, don't tell anyone about this. But go straight to the priest and let him examine you; then in order to prove to everyone that you are cured offer the sacrifice that Moses ordered."

But the man went away and began to spread the news everywhere. Indeed, he talked so much that Jesus could not go into a town publicly. Instead, he stayed out in lonely places, and people came to him from everywhere.

Mark 1:40–45

1 Tone up

Stand upright and bend to the left so that your hand goes down your side toward your knee, then straighten up and do the same to the right. 10 times. Lie on your front and push yourself up off the ground with your hands. 6 times. Then sit down in a circle round the chart.

2 All quiet

Your leader will say a prayer that everyone will understand today's Bible story. Then he or she will choose someone to read what happened when Jesus met someone whom no one liked.

Sick people are sometimes still healed today when Christians pray for them. If it is God's plan for them to be well again, he will work alongside doctors and medicine to heal them. Ask your leader if he or she has known this to happen.

28

People with the disease leprosy were sent away from home. No one went near them for fear of catching the disease. What kinds of people today can you think of whom everyone avoids?

What does it tell you about Jesus that he was willing to touch a person that no one else would go near?

How would Jesus react to the people on the list you have just made?

4 Body stretch

If you know some people who are ill, write their names here.

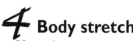

Say some prayers for them asking God to heal them.

DAY 3

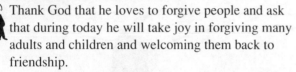

Left leg day

THINGS GO WRONG AND I NEED FORGIVENESS
Luke 7:36–50; 15:11–24

9.30 / 6.15
LEADERS' PREPARATION

Thank God that he loves to forgive people and ask that during today he will take joy in forgiving many adults and children and welcoming them back to friendship.

Read Luke 7:36–50 and 15:11–24, then discuss some or all of these questions:

1 Although it is always assumed that the woman was repentant, she does not actually say anything throughout the passage. What makes us sure that she wanted forgiveness?

2 If the woman was forgiven without saying a word, could it be that some children can be forgiven by God without saying a word? Or should we ask them to say a particular prayer and follow a set formula?

3 What does Luke 15:20–24 reveal to us about God's nature?

4 How can this parable motivate us to love and help the children at this club?

Hold a silence in which individuals can speak to God about their own need for forgiveness, then suggest that each group leader reads the names of all the children in his or her group, asking for God's love to captivate them.

10.15 / 6.30
PREVIEW

Welcome children, register them, and take them to their groups. On today's badge, children should draw and colour things they enjoy doing – their favourite activities, toys, games, outings and entertainments. If children are making their own badges as well as drawing them, suggest that they make crazy shapes for them – stars, triangles, bottles, crescents, trees, etc.

10.30 / 6.45
WARM UP

Sing the *Bodybuilders* song, use the catch-phrase, and so on.

10.35 / 6.50
FUN RUN

The leader should take off his or her shoes to reveal a bare foot. The group then turns the foot into a face, using make-up left over from Day 1, wool for hair, paper and *Sellotape* for ears and so on. After a three minute time limit, ask the leaders to show off their feet and lead a cheer for each foot–face in turn.

10.40 / 6.55
AEROBICS

Some more simple exercises, making special use of the head and face.

10.44 / 6.59
TANNOY I

All are the same. All people have sinned and are not good enough for God's glory. People are made right with God by his grace, which is a free gift. (From Romans 3: 22–23)

10.45 / 7.00
TEAM TALK

Isn't God terrific! He made us, he loves us, he listens to us when we pray, he gives us what is good for us. Surely there cannot be a better way to live than to try to please him in all we do!

Well, of course that's true. But sometimes we don't live that way. Sometimes we fight or hurt or argue with the other people whom God loves just as much. Sometimes we spoil the world God has made for us to use and enjoy by polluting it, or ill-treating it or destroying its resources. And sometimes, because we are selfish or cruel, we act as if God wasn't even there, or as if we had left him and run away to do just what we please. I wonder how he feels when that happens? I wonder whether he stops loving us? Here's a made-up story:

'Goodbye Dad'

'Goodbye son. Take care how you go. Don't forget me.' And Joe ran off down the path away from home. He didn't look back; he just kept walking. In his suitcase was everything he owned. He had asked his father to give him the share of the money he would receive in his will, and his father had done so. And now Joe felt on top of the world – rich, excited… and free! Was it wrong to leave home so soon? Joe knew how hurt his dad would feel – maybe even angry. But he was fed up with keeping his father's rules, and away he went.

He caught the train to Big City and started the wildest time in his whole life. He did what he pleased, when he pleased, how he pleased. And if it cost a fortune, he didn't care! And if it caused misery to other people, he didn't care! And if he knew what he was doing was wrong, he didn't care. He had money, he had friends, he had good times.

But he never stopped to think that one day the money would run out. One dismal day, it did! And he never thought that when the money ran out, his friends would lose interest in him. One dismal day they did! And he never realized that when his friends lost interest, the good times would come to an end. One dismal day, they did! He was broke, alone, and very miserable.

He tried to get a job to make ends meet, but the only job he could get was on a pig farm, sweeping up what was left when the pigs had finished eating. The smell was awful, the pay was lousy and no one seemed to care. And as he sat in the pig pen, lonely as could be, he thought for the first time in months of his father and his home. And he made a decision. He would walk back down the highway (he couldn't afford a coach ticket), go to his father's door and say, 'Dad, I'm sorry. I shouldn't have left you. I shouldn't have done wrong. I don't suppose you want me back as a son. Please could I come and work for you as a servant?'

It was a long, tiring journey. By the time he got home his clothes were torn, he was filthy and looked unlovable. As he turned the corner of the familiar street he wondered. 'What will Dad say? Will he turn me away? Will he declare that he can never forgive me? Will he …?'

Joe couldn't believe his eyes? From the far end of the street his father was running. Running towards him; hurtling towards him with his arms outstretched.

His dad flung his arms round him and before Joe had time to stammer out, 'Sorry'. His father said, 'Joe I'm so pleased to see you. I love you so much. Come inside; there's a welcome home party ready for you right now!'

You know, God is like that father. No matter how many wrong things we have done, he is longing to say, 'I forgive you. Welcome home!' If we say sorry to him – and we all need to, adults and children alike – he says, 'That's OK. I'm glad you're sorry, I forgive you. Let's be friends.'

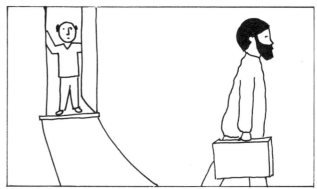

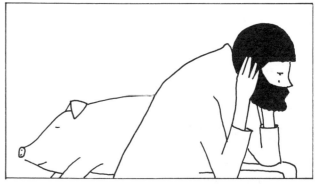

`10.50` `7.05` WORK OUT

Colour and add detail to the poster of the left leg and put it in position below the left arm.

5–7s: Cut out the six cards which are provided on page 33 so that they can be placed face down in the centre of the circle. Give one child a die and invite him or her to throw it. If a five or six is thrown, the child turns over the top card. If a one, two, three or four is thrown, the child passes the die to the next person. Every time a card is turned up, the leader reads it and shows the picture. The group must decide which person on the card has done wrong and needs to say sorry to God. The child who turned the card over may have the first chance to speak, if he or she wishes to. After each short discussion, the leader should remind the group that God will always forgive those who say sorry to him, circle the name of the person chosen, and attach the card inside the leg with the caption: 'God longs to forgive....'

8–11s: Brainstorm things that people do which are sinful and that hurt God. Prompt a wide range of replies, including not only personal failures (such as lying or stealing), but world wide failures (such as allowing the ozone layer to be destroyed, or drug smuggling). As these are suggested, the leader should write each one on a separate file card and toss it on the floor. When there are no more ideas, ask the group to work together to sort the file–cards into three piles – sins which are more likely to be committed by children, those which are more likely to be committed by adults, and those to which children and adults are both equally susceptible. When this has been done, the leader should remind the group that God will always forgive those who say sorry to him, be they young or old. Attach the cards inside the leg with the caption: 'God longs to forgive....'

`11.10` `7.25` TANNOY 2

There is no God like you. You forgive people who are guilty of sin. You, Lord, will not stay angry for ever. You enjoy being kind. Lord, you will have mercy on us again. You will throw away all our sins into the deepest sea. (From Micah 7:18–19)

`11.11` `7.26` LAP OF HONOUR

Songs of praise to God, adding perhaps one new song about forgiveness to those already familiar. Suitable songs would be 'God is so good' or 'Cleanse me from my sin, Lord'. After a quieter song, the presenter should introduce a time of silence (about ten or twelve seconds) by saying that if anyone, adult or child, wants to say sorry to God for anything they have done which has let him down, they can do so and he will completely forgive them. Stress that God will listen and understand, even though they do not say any words aloud. After the silence, use this chant. Establish a rhythm by clicking fingers and say the words together rhythmically four times, getting louder each time until a final joyful shout. The clicks are on God, God, God, now:

> God is great,
> God is loving,
> God forgives us now,
> Yeah!

`11.20` `7.35` EXTRA TIME

Either craft activities or Bible-reading posters (5–7s on pages 34–35, 8–11s on pages 36–37).

`11.45` `8.00` ACTION REPLAY

The script for part 3 of the soap opera is on page 60.

`11.55` `8.10` SHAKE OUT

Give announcements, use the catch-phrase, and say goodbye by challenging everyone to shake elbows with as many people as possible in sixty seconds.

`12.00` `8.15` CRASH OUT

After the children have left, gather the leaders and ask them each to share with the others one thing they are hoping for in the second half of the week – it could be concerning a particular child, an activity, or their whole group. Spend time praying that God will fulfil these hopes in a way which pleases him, then prepare for Day 4.

YOU WILL NEED:

At the door:
- Registration forms
- Pen

Presenter's area:
- Overhead projector
- Acetates: words of songs and illustrations
- Sound system

- Cassette player and cassettes of tannoy messages, aerobics music and phone ringing
- Soap opera properties
- Detailed forms
- Felt-tipped pens
- Left-over make-up, wool, paper, etc
- Left leg poster, felt marker, *Blu-Tack*
- Situation cards, dice (5–7s)
- File cards, pens (8–11s)
- Craft equipment or Bible-reading posters

In groups:

- Blue or black belts
- Badges or card, scissors, *Sellotape*, safety pins

There was a new girl in the class. She had a squeaky voice which was different from anyone else. At playtime Daniel said everyone should play with her. Tanya said she didn't want to because she didn't like her voice.

Paul and Damien were playing with their cars. Paul threw his car in the air and it knocked a vase over. Mum heard the noise and came running. Paul said, 'Damien did it'.

Mrs Jones promised that if the class worked really hard they could go outside and play games in the afternoon. Jenny did her best writing ever and worked as hard as she could. She asked Mrs Jones if they could play games. Mrs Jones said, 'No, I've changed my mind'.

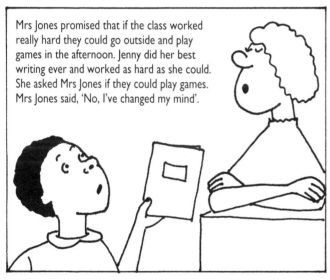

Dad gave Donny a bag of sweets and said, 'Share them with Lucy'. When Dad went back into the house, Donny went and hid behind a wall. He ate them all. Lucy cried.

When Mr Carpenter said it was time to line up at the door, Shelley beat Ramish to the front of the queue. Ramish was fed up. When Mr Carpenter wasn't looking, he gave Shelley a really big pinch.

It was a sunny afternoon and lots of people were having a picnic up on Woody Hill. The White family left empty drink bottles and wrappers behind on the grass when they went home. The Hudson family put their wrappers in the waste bin and took their bottles away to be recycled and used again.

See WORK OUT 5–7s on page 32

DAY 3
Blue belts

1 Tone up

Lie down on your back and lift your legs in the air as high as they will go. 10 times. Then sit in a circle round the chart.

2 All quiet

Your leader will say a prayer, then he or she will read you a story about Jesus meeting a sad woman. Look at the pictures.

3 Muscle builder

A Pharisee invited Jesus to have dinner with him, and Jesus went to his house and sat down to eat.

In that town was a woman who lived a sinful life. She heard that Jesus was eating in the Pharisee's house, so she brought an alabaster jar full of perfume and stood behind Jesus, by his feet, crying and wetting his feet with her tears. Then she dried his feet with her hair, kissed them, and poured the perfume on them. When the Pharisee saw this, he said to himself. "If this man really were a prophet, he would know who this woman is who is touching him; he would know what kind of sinful life she lives!"

34

"You are right," said Jesus. Then he turned to the woman and said to Simon, "Do you see this woman? I came into your home, and you gave me no water for my feet, but she has washed my feet with her tears and dried them with her hair. You did not welcome me with a kiss, but she has not stopped kissing my feet since I came. You provided no olive-oil for my head, but she has covered my feet with perfume. I tell you, then, the great love she has shown proves that her many sins have been forgiven. But whoever has been forgiven little shows only a little love."

Then Jesus said to the woman, "Your sins are forgiven." The others sitting at the table began to say to themselves, "Who is this, who even forgives sins?" But Jesus said to the woman, "Your faith has saved you; go in peace."

4 Body stretch

We don't know what the woman had done that was wrong. What sort of things do you think it might have been? Give your leader some ideas and he or she will write them in this space.

Have a little silence during which everyone can think whether there is anything for which they need to say sorry to God. Then the leader will say, 'Please forgive us, Lord God. Amen'.

God loves to forgive every single person who says sorry to him because he loves them. Everyone in the group should put a tick in one of these circles, because God loves every single one of you.

35

DAY 3
Black belts

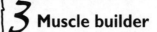

3 Muscle builder

A Pharisee invited Jesus to have dinner with him, and Jesus went to his house and sat down to eat. In that town was a woman who lived a sinful life. She heard that Jesus was eating in the Pharisee's house, so she brought an alabaster jar full of perfume and stood behind Jesus, by his feet, crying and wetting his feet with her tears. Then she dried his feet with her hair, kissed them, and poured the perfume on them. When the Pharisee saw this, he said to himself, "If this man really were a prophet, he would know who this woman is who is touching him; he would know what kind of sinful life she lives!"

Because it was a hot, dusty country, when you had guests to dinner, you got a servant to wash their feet. Simon didn't, but this woman did in a surprising way.

1 Tone up

Clasp your hands together and jump or step through the loop it makes, then step back again. 3 times. Lie on your side and lift your right leg as high as it will go. 8 times for each leg. Then sit down in a circle round the chart.

"You are right," said Jesus. Then he turned to the woman and said to Simon, "Do you see this woman? I came into your home, and you gave me no water for my feet, but she has washed my feet with her tears and dried them with her hair. You did not welcome me with a kiss, but she has not stopped kissing my feet since I came. You provided no olive-oil for my head, but she has covered my feet with perfume. I tell you, then, the great love she has shown proves that her many sins have been forgiven. But whoever has been forgiven little shows only a little love."

Then Jesus said to the woman, "Your sins are forgiven." The others sitting at the table began to say to themselves, "Who is this, who even forgives sins?" But Jesus said to the woman, "Your faith has saved you; go in peace."

Luke 7:36–39;44–50

2 All quiet

Someone should say a prayer asking Jesus to be with you, even though you can't see him, as you read the Bible. Then read what happened to Jesus.

36

We don't know what the woman had done that was sinful. Write some things down that you think it might have been.

→

4 Body stretch

Have a little silence during which everyone can think whether there is anything for which they need to say sorry to God. Then on the count of three (by the leader), everyone can say:

Lord God, forgive me. Amen.

The leader will say a prayer thanking God that he has forgiven and forgotten our sins. Then say other prayers if you want to.

Why do you think it is so important to have your sins forgiven? Would it matter if you just ignored God's offer to forgive you and carried on?
Write some ideas in the space.

→

DAY 4

Right arm day

GOD STEPPED INTO OUR WORLD IN JESUS
1 John 4:9–10, Acts 2:22–24, Luke 18:35–43

🕘 9.30 6.15
LEADERS' PREPARATION

Pray that Jesus will become more real to and more fully understood by every adult and child in the club today.

Read 1 John 4:9–10, Acts 2:22–24 and Luke 18:35–43, then discuss some or all of these questions:

1 Do you find it hard to believe that Jesus was once the same age as the children in the club? Why or why not?

2 If Jesus asked you, 'What do you want me to do for you?', as he did in Luke 18:41, what would you reply? And what do you most want him to do for the children?

3 What would the world have lost if Jesus had not come to our planet?

4 What most attracts you to the character of Jesus? What will most attract the children? Pray that Jesus will come alive to children both as a historical figure and a living person. Pray for all the leaders who will be Jesus' representatives today – ask for wisdom to be good ambassadors.

🕙 10.15 6.30
PREVIEW

Welcome children, register them, and take them to their groups. On today's badge, children should draw and colour their favourite foods and drinks. If children are making their own badges as well as drawing them, they could be made in the shape of dinner plates, and knives and forks made of aluminium foil could be added to the badge.

🕥 10.30 6.45
WARM UP

Sing the *Bodybuilders* song, use the catch-phrase, and so on.

🕥 10.35 6.50
FUN RUN

Put the group in pairs. They are to sit cross-legged on the floor, with one hand behind their backs and the other clenched into a fist. Give each pair two grapes. Every child must hold a grape between his or her clenched fist and the partner's forehead. Without dropping the grapes or using either hand to help, they must stand up, walk around the circle, and sit cross-legged again. They may eat whatever is left of the grapes!

🕥 10.40 6.55
AEROBICS

Simple exercises, drawing particular attention to arms.

🕥 10.44 6.59
TANNOY I

This is how God showed his love to us: he sent his only Son into the world to give us life through him. True love is God's love for us, not our love for God. God sent his Son to be the way to take away our sins. (1 John 4: 9–10)

🕥 10.45 7.00
TEAM TALK

We know that God made our planet. We know that he loves our planet. Do you know that God has visited our planet?

When he realized that men and women, boys and girls, were not living the way he planned, that they were doing wrong and ignoring him, God made a decision to do something absolutely wonderful and world-changing. He decided to send his only Son to live on our planet, Earth. He chose the best time – about two thousand years ago; he chose the best place – a small, green, comfortable country by the sea

called Israel; he chose the best family – a young man and woman who lived and worked in a historic village. There a baby was born who was God's very own Son. I expect you know his name – it is Jesus. You may have been learning about him in 'Extra Time'. On Christmas Day it is his coming into the world that we celebrate.

The baby grew into a fine young man. His first job was as a carpenter, making things out of wood. But when he was about thirty, he set off on a new job – a travelling job, going round the country of Israel telling people about God. He told them God made the world, that he loved them, that they could pray to him, asking him for things or saying thank you or sorry. How strange – almost exactly the same things as the leaders have been telling you about God this week!

However, there was one big difference. Quite unlike any other human before or since, Jesus was completely perfect. He never did anything wrong, although I am sure he was very often tempted to. Instead, he went about doing good. He made a point of making friends with those who felt lonely or left out. He was particularly full of love for the sick, and often he would make them better in dramatic and remarkable ways. Children in particular loved him. Wherever he went, men and women would follow him enthusiastically, and they would find their lives were transformed by the good he brought out in them. He was the loveliest man who ever lived. He was God's own!

He was so popular, however, that the rulers of the country found him threatening. They were afraid that he would take over the country and get rid of them – quite wrongly of course. And so they sent soldiers to arrest him, put him on trial for a crime he never committed, and had him put to death – by hanging him on a wooden cross. It was a terrible thing to do.

But Jesus was God's own Son. And he was not only a good man and a great teacher, he had all the power that God could give him. He was more powerful even than death. Three days after he died, he came back to life again, completely triumphant. On Easter Sunday, it is his return to life that we celebrate. Those who followed him saw him, heard him tell them to go throughout the world spreading the good news that he is alive, and saw him return to live with God in heaven.

For two thousand years, people have been taking the good news about Jesus from country to country. From a handful of people following him, the number has grown to millions and millions. They know that God has forgiven them and that just as Jesus was specially close to his father God, they too can be friends of God, now and forever. They 'follow' Jesus by trying to live as he lived. And the good news has even reached this country. And now it's being passed on to you!

All the leaders of *Bodybuilders* are Christians. They would love to tell you why they follow Jesus and how it feels to be a friend of God. Why not ask them!

See page 46 for illustrations for this talk

10.50 7.05

WORK OUT

Colour and add detail to the poster of the right arm and put it in position.

5–7s: Give every child a photocopy of the balloon containing a picture of Jesus (page 41). Describe what is going on in the picture. Remind the children of what Jesus invited his friends to do by helping them join the dots and make the words 'Follow me'. Then give the children felt-tipped pens and encourage them to colour the picture, adding features to the faces of Jesus' friends. While this low-key activity is taking place, the leader could take the opportunity to chat one-to-one with the children about what Jesus means to him or her.

8–11s: Give every child a photocopy of the balloon containing two matching pictures of events outside the tomb (page 41). Explain that it shows what astonished Mary, one of Jesus' closest followers, when she came to visit his grave – he was alive! Show the children a Bible and explain that all the truths about God and Jesus his Son, which have been explained this week, are written down in that book. Read them the story contained in John 20:1–18. Then invite them to try to spot the differences. There are eleven (twelve if the change of words is counted: Jesus has replaced the guard, Mary's expression, her spice jar, her sandals, Simon and John leaving, the stone rolled away, crosses have gone, gate of the city, sun rising, flowers gone, mouse's tail moved). When they have done this, give the children felt-tipped pens and invite them to colour only the event that really took place. While they do this low-key activity, the leader could take the opportunity to chat one-to-one with the children about what Jesus means to him or her.

In both cases the balloons should be cut out and string attached with *Sellotape*. The balloons can be arranged around the body as if they are being held in the right hand.

39

11.10 7.25

TANNOY 2

 If anyone belongs to Jesus, then he is made new. The old things have gone; everything is made new! All this is from God. Through Jesus, God made peace between us and himself. (From 2 Corinthians 5:17–18)

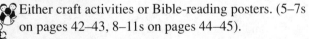 **11.11** 7.26

LAP OF HONOUR

Songs of praise which mention Jesus as well as God, adding one or two to those which are already familiar. Particularly suitable are 'Jesus' love is very wonderful', 'There is singing in the desert', or 'I'm special because God has loved me'. At some point during this section, use this prayer, with the children repeating each line after the leader:

Thank you, God, for sending Jesus.…
Thank you, God, that he lived a perfect life.…
Thank you, God, that he died on a cross.…
Thank you, God, that he rose from the dead.…
Thank you, God, that he lives forever.…
Thank you, God, that he has turned us from enemies
   into his friends.…
Jesus, you are the best ever.…

Ask everyone to think how they would finish the sentence, 'Lord Jesus, you are ....' After a moment to decide on an honest ending, invite them to tell the person sitting next to them what they decided. Then introduce a shout of praise to God, with everyone declaring together, 'Lord Jesus, you are ....' and completing the sentence in their own way. Point out that the prayer was so loud and chaotic that no one in the room heard the words, but God is so huge and powerful that he heard everyone and enjoyed the praise.

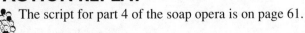 **11.20** 7.35

EXTRA TIME

Either craft activities or Bible-reading posters. (5–7s on pages 42–43, 8–11s on pages 44–45).

11.45 8.00

ACTION REPLAY

The script for part 4 of the soap opera is on page 61.

 11.55 8.10

SHAKE OUT

Give announcements, use the catch-phrase, and say goodbye by challenging everyone to shake shoulders with as many people as possible in sixty seconds.

 12.00 8.15

CRASH OUT

After the children have left, gather the leaders and ask them to evaluate the day and suggest what they would like the rest of the group to pray for. Hold a time of silence during which the leaders are to shut their eyes and imagine what they were doing with their group one hour previously, be it good or bad, thrilling or disappointing. As they think about this, they are to imagine that Jesus walked into the room in person. Invite them in their mind's eye to introduce each child in their group to Jesus. After this silent meditation, the leader should thank Jesus that he has been present in the room at every moment during the day. Commit Day 5 to him, then prepare for it.

YOU WILL NEED:

At the door:
- Registration forms
- Pen

Presenter's area:
- Overhead projector
- Acetates: words of songs and illustrations
- Sound system
- Cassette player and cassettes of tannoy messages, aerobics music and phone ringing
- Soap opera properties

In groups:
- Blue or black belts
- Badges, or card, scissors, *Sellotape*, safety pins, aluminium foil, paste
- Detailed forms
- Felt-tipped pens
- Seedless grapes
- Right leg poster, felt marker, *Blu-Tack*, balloon pictures, crayons, scissors, string (5–7s), balloon puzzles, crayons, scissors, string (8–11s)
- Craft equipment or Bible-reading posters.

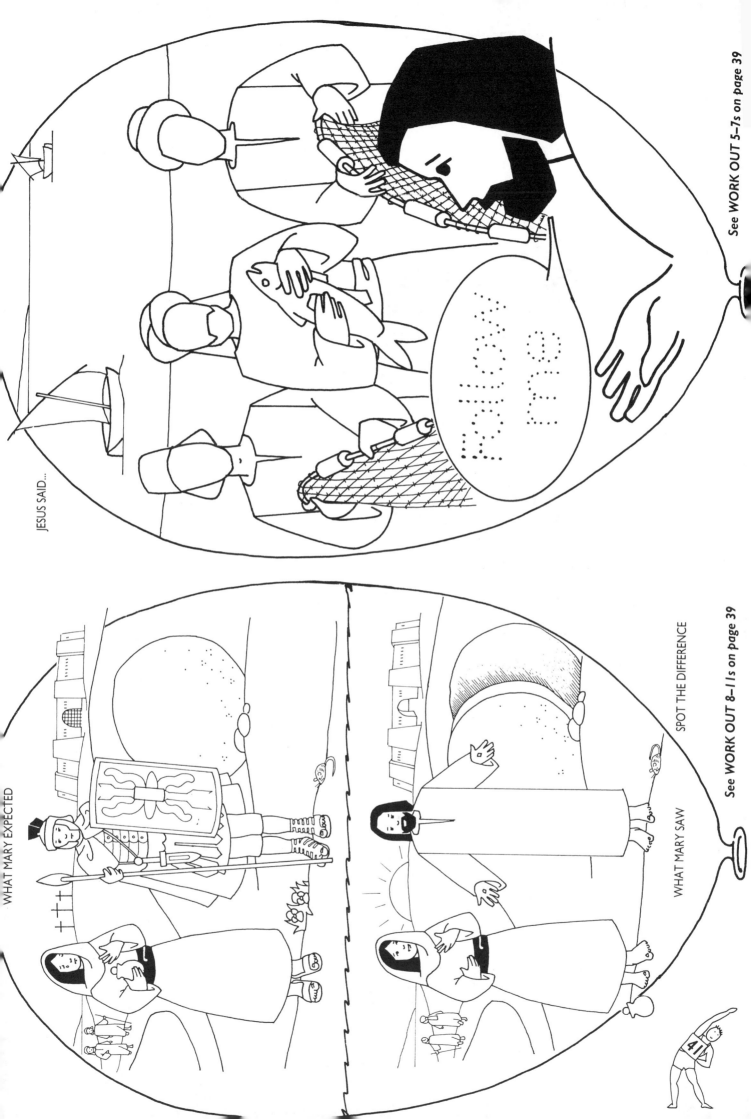

JESUS SAID...

See WORK OUT 5–7s on page 39

WHAT MARY EXPECTED

WHAT MARY SAW

SPOT THE DIFFERENCE

See WORK OUT 8–11s on page 39

41

DAY 4
Blue belts

3 Muscle builder

As Jesus was coming near Jericho, there was a blind man sitting by the road, begging. When he heard the crowd passing by, he asked, "What is this?" "Jesus of Nazareth is passing by," they told him. He cried out, "Jesus! Son of David! Take pity on me!"

The people in front scolded him and told him to be quiet. But he shouted even more loudly, "Son of David! Take pity on me!"

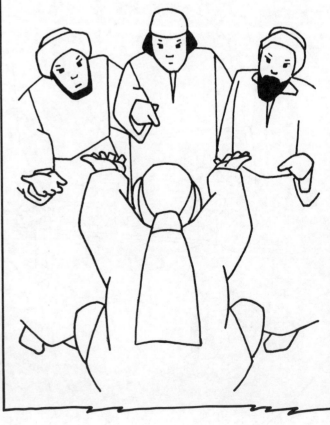

1 Tone up

March up and down on the spot. As you lift your knee each time, touch it with your hand. 20 times. Then sit in a circle round the chart.

2 All quiet

Your leader will say a prayer thanking God that all the stories in the Bible are true. They listen to another story which shows how amazing Jesus was.

So Jesus stopped and ordered the blind man to be brought to him. When he came near, Jesus asked him, "What do you want me to do for you?" "Sir," he answered, "I want to see again."

Jesus said to him, "Then see! Your faith has made you well."

At once he was able to see, and he followed Jesus, giving thanks to God. When the crowd saw it, they all praised God.

4 Body stretch

How do you think the man felt after Jesus had healed him? Talk about it for a bit, then everyone can draw a face to show how the man felt. Don't forget to give him big eyes which can see clearly.

When everyone has drawn a face, talk about what you feel about Jesus, now you know some of the things he did. Your leader will say a prayer telling Jesus how special he is, using some of your words.

DAY 4
Black belts

1 Tone up

Lie on your back, bring your knees up to your chest and stretch them again. 10 times. Stand up and touch your toes. 12 times. Then sit down in a circle round the chart.

Because the man was blind there was no job he could do – unlike today. The only way to survive was to beg.

3 Muscle builder

As Jesus was coming near Jericho, there was a blind man sitting by the road, begging. When he heard the crowd passing by, he asked, "What is this?"

"Jesus of Nazareth is passing by," they told him.

He cried out, "Jesus! Son of David! Take pity on me!"

The people in front scolded him and told him to be quiet. But he shouted even more loudly, "Son of David! Take pity on me!"

So Jesus stopped and ordered the blind man to be brought to him. When he came near, Jesus asked him, "What do you want me to do for you?"

"Sir," he answered, "I want to see again."

Jesus said to him, "Then see! Your faith has made you well."

At once he was able to see, and he followed Jesus, giving thanks to God. When the crowd saw it, they all praised God.

Luke 18:35–43

Why do you think the man followed after Jesus down the road?

2 All quiet

Anyone who wants to can pray that you will all enjoy reading part of the Bible today. Then another person can read the story to you all.

44

What do you think it feels like to be blind? What would you miss most?
Shut your eyes and try to write your name in this space.

�**4 Body stretch**

Think of some things which you would really like to happen during the days and weeks ahead. Tell God about them in a prayer if you want to.
Begin it:

Please God, ...
Amen.

Then your leader will say a prayer.

See TEAM TALK on pages 38, 39

46

DAY 5
Right leg day

FOLLOWING JESUS IS THE BEST WAY TO LIVE
Romans 15:1–6, Luke 19:1–10

9.30 6.15
LEADERS' PREPARATION

 Pray that one of the results of this week will be that the church will become more united as you seek to follow Christ.

Read Romans 15:1–6 and Luke 19:1–10, then discuss some or all of these questions.

1 What does Romans 15:1–6 suggest that your team will need in order to achieve unity?

2 What are the principle ways in which we should 'follow the example of Christ Jesus' according to this passage? If Paul had added a paragraph about what it means for children to follow Christ's example, what might he have suggested?

3 Is there any kind of child who we tend to assume is, like Zacchaeus in Luke 19:1–10, impossibly unlikely to respond to Jesus?

4 How do we know Zacchaeus' change was genuine, and what can we learn about what Jesus looks for in his followers?

Pray that, in God's time and in God's way, the children at the club will become changed people. Pray for continued contact with children beyond this final day.

10.15 6.30
PREVIEW

Welcome children, register them and take them to their groups. On today's badge, children should draw something that represents their favourite programmes on television. If children are making their own badges as well as drawing them, they could be made in the shape of television sets, with the pictures drawn on the 'screen' area.

10.30 6.45
WARM UP

 Sing the *Bodybuilders* song and use the catch-phrase. Point out that today is the final day of *Bodybuilders* (booooo!), but that everyone is welcome to come back with their families to the all-age service (hurray!).

10.35 6.50
FUN RUN

Sit the group in a circle and ask them to take off their shoes and socks. Put a cellophane-wrapped sweet in front of each child. Using only their toes, they must unwrap the sweet and put it into the mouth of the person on the left. Everyone does this at the same time.

10.40 6.55
AEROBICS

 Simple exercises, drawing particular attention to legs.

10.44 6.59
TANNOY 1

 This is how we know that we are following God; whoever says that God lives in him must live as Jesus lived. God sent his Son to be the way to take away our sins. That is how much God loved us, dear friends! So we must also love each other. (From 1 John 2:5–6; 4:10–11)

10.45 7.00
TEAM TALK

 When God sent Jesus to our earth, he did everything that was needed for us to be friends with him. No matter whether we are tall or small, he loves us. No matter whether we have done many things wrong or just a few, he forgives us when we say sorry. No

47

matter whether we are clever or confused, he lets us follow him as his friends. Wow!

God knows the best way for us to live our lives – of course he does, for he designed our world and understands precisely how it works. The best way to live is to be like Jesus, and that is how he wants us to be. Someone who brings peace when it would be easy to argue or fight. Someone who doesn't give in to doing wrong, even when the temptation is great. Someone who is prepared to love others, even when that makes life awkward. Someone who is prepared to protect God's world, even when that makes them unpopular. My word, these are hard things to do, and only God's help will allow us to do them! For all of us, man or woman, boy or girl, being God's friend means change!

Let me tell you a story. In a distant country of the world called India there was a doctor. India is not like this country. In some places there is only one doctor covering many, many miles of mountainous land, where hazardous tracks across the slopes connect villages. This was just such a doctor.

He was about to close his clinic on a weary Friday afternoon when there was a knock on the door. When he opened it, he saw an old man who was obviously in great pain. 'Please can you help me,' begged the man. 'I have walked 40 kilometres from my mountain village because they said you would help.' The doctor looked down at the man's feet. They were ruined with disease – swollen, bleeding, covered with sores. His heart melted. 'Come in', he said simply.

The doctor worked on the man's feet for over an hour, cleaning them, rubbing in ointment and bandaging them. 'Your feet will be well again now', he explained kindly. 'However, there is something you must do.' He went to a shelf at the back of the clinic and got down a box. 'I am going to give you a change of shoes. You must always, always, always wear these shoes. Then your feet will be protected and they will always be well.'

The man's eyes lit up. When he tried on the shoes he could barely contain his gratitude. He said thank you again and again. And with a much easier and more comfortable stride, he went on his way.

Some months later the doctor decided to make a visit to the villages remote in the mountains. He packed up his medicines and surgical tools and set off with his mobile clinic. You can imagine his delight when, as he entered one village, he saw the man whose feet he treated. He was about to greet him as an old friend when .... surely not .... he could barely believe it .... he saw the man hobbling towards him painfully on bare feet – swollen, bleeding, covered in sores.

The doctor was almost in tears. 'But .... but where .... where are your shoes?'

The old man smiled and beckoned. 'Come with me', he said, limping slowly and pitifully toward his home. 'Come inside.' From under the bed he took a beautifully carved wooden box and opened it up. There inside, wrapped in cotton, were the doctor's shoes. 'These shoes are my most precious possessions in the world', said the man proudly. 'They are so special that I keep them safe with the most valuable things I own. I wear them without fail .... every Sunday.'

Oh dear! That was no good at all, was it? When the doctor said change, he meant the man had to change for the whole of his life. And when God asks us to change, he means he wants us to change the whole of our lives. Just like you and I are utterly special to him, he wants to be utterly special to us. Not just one day of the week, not just during the *Bodybuilders* week, but all the time. I wonder whether you feel ready to make a change like that. Some of you may; some of you will want to think about it for longer.

God is a friend who will stay by you through good times and bad for ever and ever. Perhaps you would like to stick with him for ever and ever as well. How will that change you?

Some illustrations for this talk can be found on page 56

10.50 7.05

WORK OUT

Colour and add detail to the poster of the right leg and put it in position, completing the building of the body.

5–7s: Give each child a piece of coloured paper and invite them to draw around their foot on it with a pencil. They should then use scissors to cut it out. Talk together about ways in which they feel they could change if they were going to follow Jesus' example, encouraging them to suggest realistic and simple ideas. Help every child to choose one and write it on his or her paper foot. They may then decorate it with felt–tipped pens and attach it with *Blu-Tack* to the poster, surrounding the feet.

8–11s: Put the group into pairs and ask them to talk together about ways in which they would want to change if they decided to follow Jesus. Each should choose one. Give them sheets of coloured paper and ask them to design and cut out 'a change of shoes' in an imaginative way for the group's body. They should write the changes they thought of on the shoes and *Blu-Tack* them to the chart.

11.10 7.25

TANNOY 2

I pray that God will help you all agree with each other the way Jesus wants. Then you will all be joined together, and you will give glory to God the father of our Lord Jesus. He accepted you, so you should accept each other. This will bring glory to God. (From Romans 15:5–7)

11.11 7.26

LAP OF HONOUR

Songs of praise which talk about our response to what Jesus has done for us, adding one or two to those which children have found thrilling during the week. Particularly suitable are 'Get up out of bed' and 'Jesus put this song into our hearts'. At some point during this, hold a time of thanksgiving. Ask the children to think for a moment, 'If you had the chance to say thank you to God right now, what is the thing you would most like to thank him for?' Invite them to tell the person sitting next to them what they have decided on – give them about fifteen seconds to do this. Then hold a time of open prayer, suggesting that any child who wishes to says, 'Thank you God for.... (whatever they have decided on)'. Stress that if two people accidentally (or intentionally) say their prayers at the same time it does not matter, because God is so powerful that he can hear everyone at the same time. The leader should say the first prayer to establish the structure, and say a loud 'Amen' after each child's contribution as a mark of affirmation.

11.20 7.35

EXTRA TIME

 Either craft activities or Bible-reading posters (5–7s on pages 50–51, 8–11s on pages 52–53).

11.45 8.00

ACTION REPLAY

The script for the final part of the soap opera is on page 62.

 11.55 8.10

SHAKE OUT

Give announcements, use the catch-phrase, remind children of the all-age service, and say goodbye by challenging everyone to shake bottoms with as many people as possible in sixty seconds. As children leave, give them invitations to the all-age service to give to those who share their homes.

 12.00 8.15

CRASH OUT

After the children have left, gather the leaders and invite them to reflect (more emotionally than evaluatively as on previous days) on how they feel about the week as a whole. In your prayers thank God for the things that have thrilled you and, if you can, thank him even for the things that have been disappointing. After this, ask God to help you learn from the disappointing things and continue to pray for the children, particularly that they and their families will attend the all-age service. Move on to prepare the service and clear up the room.

YOU WILL NEED:

At the door:
- Registration forms
- Pen
- Invitations to the all-age service

Presenters' area:
- Overhead projector
- Acetates: words of songs and illustrations
- Sound system
- Cassette player and cassettes of tannoy messages, aerobics music and phone ringing
- Soap opera properties

In groups:
- Blue or black belts, which may be taken away at the end
- Badges, or card, scissors, *Sellotape*, safety pins
- Detailed forms
- Wrapped sweets
- Right leg poster, felt marker, *Blu-Tack*, coloured paper, pencils, felt-tipped pens, craft equipment or
- Bible-reading posters.

DAY 5
Blue belts

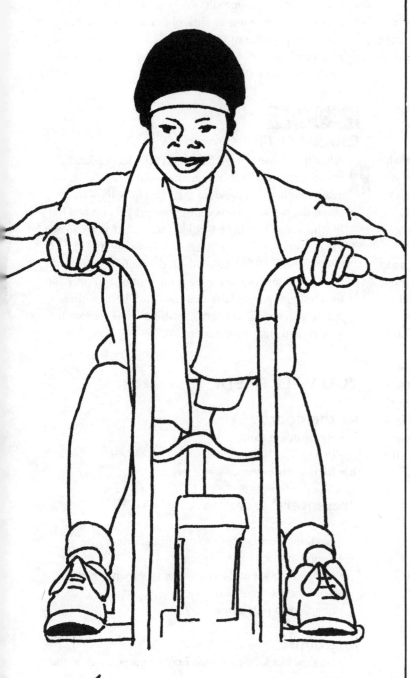

1 Tone up

Find a big space and swing your arms round in a big circle. 5 times forwards. 5 times backwards. 5 times forwards. 5 times backwards. Then sit in a circle round the chart.

2 All quiet

After saying a prayer, listen to this Bible story about Jesus and a man whom no one liked.

3 Muscle builder

Jesus went on into Jericho and was passing through. There was a chief tax collector there named Zacchaeus, who was rich. He was trying to see who Jesus was, but he was a little man and could not see Jesus because of the crowd.

So he ran ahead of the crowd and climbed a sycamore tree to see Jesus, who was going to that place, he looked up and said to Zacchaeus, "Hurry down, Zacchaeus, because I must stay in your house today."

50

Zacchaeus hurried down and welcomed him with great joy. All the people who saw it started grumbling, "This man has gone as a guest to the home of a sinner!"

Zacchaeus stood up and said to the Lord, "Listen, sir! I will give half my belongings to the poor, and if I have cheated anyone, I will pay him back four times as much."

4 Body stretch

Has there ever been a time when you were too small to see and everyone else was big? Talk about that time to the group. Then talk about how you think Zacchaeus felt when he wanted to see Jesus.

Whether you are big or small or in between, God likes you just the way you are. Write the names of everyone in the group on the leaves below.

Zacchaeus

Say some prayers so that you tell God about every person in the group. If anyone would like to pray about something special, tell your leader now. Then he or she will explain how you are going to pray.

51

Black belts

1 Tone up

Stand up straight. Bend over and touch your left foot
with your right hand and lift your left arm in the air.
Then do the opposite with your left hand. 12 times.
Lie on your back with your legs bent and your knees
in the air. Sit up and touch your knees with your nose.
then lie back again. 4 times. Then sit down in a circle
round the chart.

Unlike today, men who
collected taxes in Jesus'
time were nearly all
cheats and everyone
hated them.

2 All quiet

Get ready to read the Bible by saying a prayer. Then
listen while someone reads about a man who changed
completely when he met Jesus.

3 Muscle builder

Jesus went on into Jericho and was passing through. There was a chief tax collector there named Zacchaeus, who was rich. He was trying to see who Jesus was, but he was a little man and could not see Jesus because of the crowd. So he ran ahead of the crowd and climbed a sycamore tree to see Jesus, who was going to pass that way. When Jesus came to that place, he looked up and said to Zacchaeus, "Hurry down, Zacchaeus, because I must stay in your house today."

Zacchaeus hurried down and welcomed him with great joy. All the people who saw it started grumbling, "This man has gone as a guest to the home of a sinner!"

Zacchaeus stood up and said to the Lord, "Listen, sir! I will give half my belongings to the poor, and if I have cheated anyone, I will pay him back four times as much."

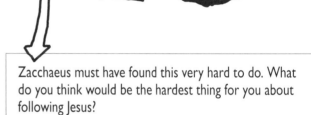

Ask your leader why he or she has decided to follow Jesus and what difference it makes to the way they live. Then anyone else who wants to can say whether they think following Jesus is a good idea – and why.

Zacchaeus must have found this very hard to do. What do you think would be the hardest thing for you about following Jesus?
Remember, if you really want to live as a follower of Jesus, God will give you all the help you need!

4 Body stretch

Stand in a circle with your arms round each others' shoulders. Everyone who wants to should pray for the person next to them. They could say:

Lord God, I pray for my friend . . . .
Amen.

or pray anything else that the person needs.

OUTLINE
All-age service

KEEP GOING WITH JESUS!

SETTING

Although the service may well take place in a different room, try to preserve some of the joyful atmosphere of the holiday club. The bodies could be displayed on the walls for the adult congregation and visitors to see. Children should be encouraged to wear their belts and the catch-phrase can be used at appropriate points in the service (taking care not to use it in a prayer or when a shouted response would be a distraction). The service should prominently involve the adults whom the children have come to know.

WELCOME AND HYMN

The leader should greet the congregation in a way that makes them feel comfortable with the slightly unusual setting. Sing a hymn which may be familiar even to visitors, but which is accessible to as many children as possible. Among suitable hymns are 'Praise my soul the King of heaven' (point out to young children then, even if they cannot manage to read the words, they can repeat 'Praise him' to Jesus many times), 'All creatures of our God and King' (which also has a refrain), or 'All things bright and beautiful'.

PRAYER

Someone should say a prayer committing your time together to God.

SONG

A leader who has been involved during the week should explain a little about what has happened, and then lead the *Bodybuilders* song. This should be interrupted in the usual way by....

TANNOY

If an athlete is running a race, he must obey the rules in order to win. There is one thing I always do: I forget the things that are past. I try as hard as I can to reach the goal that is before me. I keep trying to reach the goal and get the prize. That prize is mine because God called me through Jesus to the life above. (From 2 Timothy 2:5, Philippians 3:13–14)

SONGS

A selection of songs which praise God, chosen from those that have been used during the week.

FUN RUN

Invite everyone who has been a leader in any capacity during the week to join you at the front. Explain that it is their turn today to take part in the fun run. It will take the form of a race out of the room you are in to an appropriate point (they should be gone about thirty seconds) and back again. Start them off in the manner of an Olympic race (perhaps using a water pistol instead of a starting pistol). While they are out of the room, tell the congregation in a conspiratorial manner that you wanted them out of the way so that you could arrange for an enormous round of applause to thank them for the time and energy they put into running the club. Suggest that the congregation greets them with an ovation when they arrive back in the room. Make this race an active visual aid which leads into the....

TALK

As the tannoy message, which came direct from the Bible, showed us, being a Christian is a bit like being an athlete in a race.

Display a copy of the cartoon of an athlete (page 55), traced on to an overhead projector acetate. The words should be written on separate slips of acetate and dropped into place as the four points of the talk are made.

- **Don't look back.** Trainers often say this to runners; it wastes valuable time and might mean losing a medal. Christians are people who have come to Jesus to ask for their sins to be forgiven, so guilt about them need never drag us back. Jesus' love is all we now need.

DON'T LOOK BACK!

FOLLOW A GOOD EXAMPLE

KEEP GOING

EVERYONE WINS THE PRIZE!

- **Follow a good example.** The example of great runners of the past – Kriss Akabusi, Roger Bannister, Mary Peters, Eric Liddell – is there to inspire today's athletes. So is the vast crowd of Christians who never gave up. Imitate them, the Bible tells us. Let us both follow good examples and set a good example, so that young and old can see why belonging to Jesus makes sense.
- **Keep going.** There is a pain barrier to the Christian life as well as in sport. A runner knows that he can't eat, drink or smoke whatever he likes; there has to be discipline too – a discipline of living as Jesus wants. Don't let him down!
- **Everyone wins the prize.** There is one big difference between a race and the Christian life. The Olympic races only gave one gold medal. However, Jesus has ensured that everyone without exception who follows him will win the prize of living with him in the joy of heaven. Christians are not in competition; they are there to encourage one another. So keep going with Jesus!

SONG

One of the more substantial songs from those sung during the holiday club.

RESPONSIVE PRAYER

Leader: When difficulties face us,
All: Help us, Lord Jesus, to keep following.
Leader: When temptations are in front of us,
All: Help us, Lord Jesus, to keep following.
Leader: When failures discourage us,
All: Help us, Lord Jesus, to keep following.
Leader: When bad news makes us doubt,
All: Help us, Lord Jesus, to keep following.
Leader: When worries make us fearful,
All: Help us, Lord Jesus, to keep following.
Leader: When tiredness makes us feel like giving up,
All: Help us, Lord Jesus, to keep following.
Leader: Until we reach the marvellous goal of eternal life with you,
All: Help us, Lord Jesus, to keep following. Amen.

FURTHER PRAYERS

Either led or spontaneous, about the needs of the world, the community and the congregation. (The leader should give specific advice about the brevity, vocabulary and audibility of these prayers.)

HYMN

Either an accessible hymn about following Jesus or the *Bodybuilders* song for a final time.

CLOSE

Lord Jesus, be behind me to forgive the faults of my past;

Lord Jesus, be beside me to encourage me as I keep going with you;
Lord Jesus, be in front of me so that I may follow your example;
Lord Jesus, be ahead of me so that I may have as my goal the joy of eternal life.
Amen.

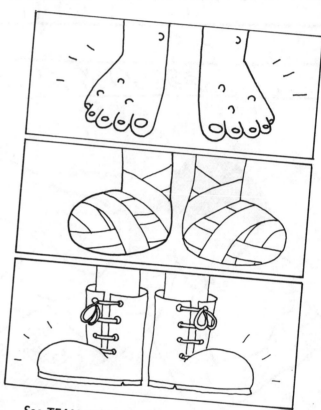

See TEAM TALK on pages 47, 48

Tannoy scripts

These scripts should be prerecorded, including the words DAY ONE, DAY TWO, etc (which are useful for cueing up but should not be 'broadcast') and the pauses … (during which children follow the instructions).

DAY ONE

… Tannoy message, tannoy message. Attention all members. Please take your seats … Here is your urgent message. God made my whole being. He formed me in my mother's body. I praise him because he made me in an amazing and wonderful way. What you have done is wonderful. All the days planned for me were written in your book before I was one day old.

… Tannoy message, tannoy message. Attention all members. Please take your seats … Here is your urgent message. Lord, you know all about me. You know when I sit down and when I get up. You know my thoughts before I think them. Even before I say a word, you already know what I am going to say. You are all around me – in front and at the back. You have put your hand on me.…

DAY TWO

… Tannoy message, tannoy message. Attention all members. Please take your seats … Here is your urgent message. The Lord is pleased with an honest person's prayer. If one of you is having troubles, he should pray. If one of you is happy he should sing praises. When a good person prays, great things happen.

… Tannoy message, tannoy message. Attention all members. Please take your seats … Here is your urgent message. Always be happy. Never stop praying. Give thanks whatever happens. That is what God wants for you in Christ Jesus.…

DAY THREE

… Tannoy message, tannoy message … Attention all members. Please take your seats… Here is your urgent message. All are the same. All people have sinned and are not good enough for God's glory. People are made right with God by his grace, which is a free gift.

… Tannoy message, tannoy message. Attention all members. Please take your seats … Here is your urgent message. There is no God like you. You forgive people who are guilty of sin. You, Lord, will not stay angry for ever. You enjoy being kind. Lord, you will have mercy on us again. You will throw away all our sins into the deepest sea.…

DAY FOUR

… Tannoy message, tannoy message … Attention all members. Please take your seats … Here is your urgent message. This is how God showed his love to us: he sent his only Son into the world to give us life through him. True love is God's love for us, not our love for God. God sent his Son to be the way to take away our sins.

… Tannoy message, tannoy message. Attention all members. Please take your seats … Here is your urgent message. If anyone belongs to Jesus, then he is made new: The old things have gone, everything is made new! All this is from God. Through Jesus, God made peace between us and himself.…

DAY FIVE

… Tannoy message, tannoy message. Attention all members. Please take your seats … Here is your urgent message. This is how we know that we are following God; whoever says that God lives in him must live as Jesus lived. God sent his Son to be the way to take away our sins. That is how much God loved us, dear friends! So we must also love each other.

… Tannoy message, tannoy message. Attention all members. Please take your seats … Here is your urgent message. I pray that God will help you all agree with each other the way Jesus wants. Then you will all be joined together, and you will give glory to God the Father of our Lord Jesus. He accepted you, so you should accept each other. This will bring glory to God.…

ALL–AGE SERVICE

… Tannoy message, tannoy message. Attention all members. Please take your seats … Here is your urgent message. If an athlete is running a race, he must obey the rules in order to win. There is one thing I always do: I forget the things that are past. I try as hard as I can to reach the goal that is before me. I keep trying to reach the goal and get the prize. That prize is mine because God called me through Jesus to the life above.…

57

Soap opera scripts

The drama is set in Bodybuilders Health Club. To one side is a reception desk on which is a telephone.
The acting space is a gym area surrounded by sports equipment of all kinds, both large and small.
The gym is miserably untidy and ramshackle.

CHARACTERS

Tracey, the glamorous 'brainless blonde' receptionist
Brad, a muscular gym instructor who fancies himself
Richard, his not-so-muscular wimp of a rival
Doris, the not-so-glamorous cleaner
Mrs Judge, from the council

EPISODE I

Tracey: *(Answering phone.)* Bodybuilders Health Club, can I help you? Yes, yes ... no, no. *(Sympathetically.)*... yes, yes ... Try lifting both arms in the air and wrapping your legs round your neck ... Triffic ... Bye! *(Brad enters, jogging and jumping.)* Good morning Brad.

Brad: Morning Tracey. What classes have I got today?

Tracey: You've got teenager tennis at ten, track training at twelve, toddlers' trampolining at two, and fatties' football at four.

Brad: Quite an easy day then. If I'd known I'd have jogged further than my daily ten miles and done 200 press–ups instead of 100. Can't let my standards slip.

Tracey: You certainly have got a very fit body as a result of it ... Lovely!

Brad: A beautiful body makes a beautiful person Tracey.

Tracey: Is that true?

Brad: A second-rate body means a second-rate person. And here to prove it is Richard Quick! *(Enter Richard, yawning.)*

Tracey: Good morning, Richard.

Richard: Is it morning already?!

Tracey: Wakey wakey Richard! You've got to take junior judo in the gym, husbands' hockey in the hall and pensioners' ping-pong in the playground.

Richard: Excuse me, I need to start with Richard's recuperation in the rest room. *(Exit.)*

Brad: That man is going to have to go. He's not up to the mark. If the inspector ever calls from the council he'll be in trouble.

Doris: *(Entering.)* If the inspector ever calls from the council we'll all be in trouble.

Tracey: Good morning, Doris!

Brad: What do you mean?

Doris: Well, look at this place. Run down, untidy, needing to be decorated.

Tracey: Oh but Doris, you clean up beautifully.

Doris: This place doesn't just need cleaning up. It needs a complete overhaul.

Tracey: Yes. *(Looking around.)* It isn't exactly a palace, is it.

Brad: Ah, but who cares what the surroundings are like, so long as the bodies are beautiful. *(He flexes his muscles. Richard comes back.)* There, what do you think of that, Richard? Have you got anything worth comparing? *(Richard flexes his muscles. They aren't so special.)* Huh! Call that muscle? I've seen more meat than that on a dirty fork. *(Richard flops in disappointment. The phone rings.)*

Tracey: Bodybuilders Health Club. Can I help you? Yes. I see. *(She stares ahead in a state of shock.)* Excuse me one moment. *(She gets up. Runs to the wall, hits her head on it. Screams. Turns in a circle three times. Flings herself at Brad and sobs. Jogs up and down on the spot. Puts the back of her hand to her forehead in despairing operatic fashion several times. Shakes her hair. Then sits down at the phone as calm as could be.)* Of course, madam. What did you say your name was again? Mrs Judge. Yes, we'll expect you on Friday. Goodbye.

Doris: What is it? What's wrong?

Tracey: It's the council. They're coming to do an inspection!

All: What!

Tracey: On Friday. A Mrs Judge is coming.

Doris: We'd better start a massive clean-up straight away. *(There is a certain amount of dashing and tidying, but they are soon fed up and slump.)*

Richard: You know, the trouble is I don't really want the place to be overhauled. I quite like it in the messy state it's in.

Doris: Let's go and get a coffee first, and have a good think about cleaning it up. *(Exit.)*

Richard: Good idea. Tracey, can I buy you a cup of coffee?

Tracey: Oh, no thank you Richard. I'm trying to keep off the caffeine.

Brad: Then can I buy you a cup of decaffeinated coffee?

Tracey: *(Swooning.)* Oh Brad. I'd love you to. *(She takes his arm and they sweep out.)*

58

Richard: (*Miserable.*) I don't know what's wrong with me. My body's second rate. The gym's run down. Nobody will let me buy them a cup of coffee. I've not got much brain. I'm half asleep in the morning. Who'd be me? Dick Quick! (*Enter Mrs Judge.*)

Mrs Judge: Excuse me! Is this Bodybuilders Health Club?

Richard: (*Down.*) Yes. Come in.

Mrs Judge: Are you all right? You look unhappy.

Richard: Oh, everyone's putting the boot in because I'm not good-looking or bright and my body's not so good. It's all: 'Kick thick Dick Quick.'

Mrs Judge: I'm so sorry. But you know, you needn't think like that.

Richard: How do you mean?

Mrs Judge: Because you're a human. You're totally unique. There's no one like you – a billion billion unique cells, muscles and genes working together in harmony. A mechanical marvel of variety, endlessly being remade from infinity to infinity, physically, mentally, emotionally. Standing in a place in earth's creation which no one has ever occupied, fulfilling a purpose only you were born to fulfil. You are a beautiful human person.

Richard: (*Gradually recovering.*) I'm a miracle.

Mrs Judge: You are! A unique, precious, irreplaceable miracle.

Richard: I'm a miracle! (*Leaping.*) I'm a miracle! I'm a miracle! (*Stopping short.*) I've just remembered! We've got to overhaul this entire gym before Friday or it will be closed down.

Mrs Judge: What makes you say that?

Richard: We're having an inspection from the council. The place needs to be spotless.

Mrs Judge: Now that would be a miracle.

Richard: What are we going to do? What are we going to do?

EPISODE 2

Tracey: (*Answering phone.*) Bodybuilders Health Club. Can I help you? Yes, yes ... no, no. (*Sympathetically.*) ... yes, yes ... Try putting your head between your thighs and wiggling your bottom ... Triffic ... Bye! (*Richard enters.*) Good morning Richard.

Richard: (*Yawning.*) Good morning.

Tracey: You look different somehow.

Richard: I don't know how! I'm still half asleep.

Tracey: Yes, but you don't look so miserable about it.

Richard: Well, I've been thinking since yesterday. Incidentally, do you know who that stranger was who came in while you were at coffee?

Tracey: Nobody came in.

Richard: Yes she did. I spoke to her.

Tracey: I'm sure there was no one here. (*Enter Doris.*) Good morning Doris. Did you see anyone come in here yesterday morning? A stranger?

Doris: No one. But I'd take cover if I were you. Brad's looking grim this morning. (*Enter Brad.*)

Tracey: Good morning, Br...

Brad: What have you done with my programme today?

Tracey: I don't know what you mean Brad!

Brad: You've double-booked me. I've got boys' badminton at eleven o'clock and veteran's vaulting in the same place at the same time. What am I supposed to do?

Doris: Couldn't you get them to jump over the badminton net?

Brad: Don't be stupid, you old clothes-horse. I'm going to look a fool. People won't notice my wonderful body because they will be laughing at me. There will be a boys' ballyhoo! There will be a wrangling of wrinklies! I'm so furious I'll have to go and do 100 sit-ups. It's all your fault, Tracey Spacey! (*Storms out. Tracey weeps.*)

Doris: Don't worry dear. I'll go and calm him down. (*Exit.*)

Richard: Oh Tracey, I'm so sorry.

Tracey: It's not your fault.

Richard: I know, but I'm still sorry for you. You're such a lovely person, and I'm sure you didn't double-book Brad deliberately.

Tracey: Oh, do you really think so?

Richard: Yes ... I ... I ... (*There is a scream and Brad crosses the stage carrying Doris, struggling in his arms.*)

Brad: Stupid woman! I'm putting you out.

Doris: Let me go! Bully! Put me down! (*They go.*)

Richard: I'd better try and rescue Doris! (*Exit.*)

Tracey: Oh how could you? After all I've done for you, Brad. How could you? (*Enter Mrs Judge.*)

Mrs Judge: Excuse me. Is it convenient for me to come in.

Tracey: Yes. (*Sobs.*) Bodybuilders Health Club (*Sob. Sob.*) Can I h–h–h–help ...

Mrs Judge: Do you have a problem? (*Tracey nods.*) I came here yesterday. I expect Richard said so, did he?

Tracey: So there was a stranger here yesterday!

Mrs Judge: What seems to be your problem?

Tracey: No one's listening to me. The gym needs completely redecorating by Friday. I'm in trouble on every side and no one's listening.

Mrs Judge: I'm always ready to listen. Tell me about it.

Tracey: Well ... I've got this boy, called Brad. He looks really great, but he's so cruel to me. He shouts at me, and sometimes he's so selfish. And when I speak to him, it's sometimes like I'm not even there.

Mrs Judge: You poor thing. We all need someone to listen to us. Someone who won't ever block their ears. You know, I hope you don't mind me saying so but the young man whom I was talking to yesterday ...

Tracey: Richard?

Mrs Judge: He was a charming young man. Not a great looker, but that's not what's at the heart of a human. He could be a great listener if you need one. But I must be going. (*Exit.*)

Tracey: What did you say your name w... She's gone. Hmm! Richard! Richard Quick! Perhaps there are qualities in him I have overlooked. (*Enter Richard carrying Doris, who has a bucket over her head.*)

Richard: It's all right Doris! You're safe now. (*He takes the bucket off her head. Her face is covered with mud.*)

Doris: Look what he did to me. Just look!

Tracey: You rescued her. Oh Richard, what a brave man you are.

Richard: Do you really think so?

Tracey: Oh yes! I never noticed how splendid you were before, Richard.

Richard: My close friends call me Dick.

Tracey: Dick!

Richard: Tracey!

Tracey: Dick!

Richard: Tracey!

Doris: They could make a film out of this! *(Richard and Tracey embrace. Brad rushes in.)*

Brad: Hah! Just what I expected! So you're going to be his chick now, are you?

Tracey: At least he's kind and supports me when I'm in difficulty.

Brad: Ugh! You make me sick, Dick Quick chick!

Doris: Hold it, everyone. This arguing is not going to get the gym cleaned by Friday.

Brad: Gym be jiggered. All I want right now is revenge. And I intend to get it!

EPISODE 3

Tracey: *(Answering phone.)* Bodybuilders Health Club. Can I help you? Yes, yes ... no, no. *(Sympathetically.)* ... yes, yes ... Try putting your left foot behind your right ear and holding your stomach in ... Triffic ... Bye! *(Enter Doris. She is using a chest expander and doing stretching exercises.)* Good morning Doris. What are you doing?

Doris: I'm going to need this. We all are. That Brad is going too far, and if he attacks me again, I'm going to be ready.

Tracey: Oh Doris, you'll look so silly. Cleaners don't have muscles like Arnold Schwarzenegger. You'll break your brooms.

Doris: Besides, if we are going to transform this place by Friday, we're all going to need to be as fit as can be. It's Wednesday already and we haven't started yet – we're still arguing.

Tracey: You're right. I'll start to help you straight away. *(She does.)*

Doris: I've developed a new system of cleaning. It's called 'keep fit and sweep grit'. I'll show you. *(She makes three sweeps of the broom, and then makes three 'weightlifting' jerks with it.)* One two three, one two three, one two three, one two three ... *(Enter Richard.)*

Richard: Doris, what are you doing?

Tracey: Good morning, Richard. She's a fitness and cleanness programme all in one.

Richard: Amazing. Are we ready to start painting yet?

Doris: We certainly are. What colour are the walls going to be?

Richard: White.

Doris: And is all the paint ready?

Richard: Ready and waiting.

Doris: Come on Tracey. Let's show these men what we can do. *(They go. Richard starts to sweep. Brad enters with a bucket in each hand and one in his teeth.)*

Brad: Hmmphumphuth!

Richard: Sorry! I can't hear a word you're saying.

Brad: Hmmphumphuth!

Richard: Hang on! Give me those. *(He takes the buckets from Brad's arms and holds one in each hand. They weigh his arms down.)*

Brad: *(Taking the other bucket from his mouth.)* I said: Are you ready for the paint yet?

Richard: Oh! yes, I'm ready.

Brad: Good. *(He takes a paintbrush out of the bucket and slaps white paint all over Richard. Doris and Tracey enter to see this.)*

Doris: Brad, what are you doing?

Tracey: Oh Dick, my poor dear. What has he done to you. *(She rushes to him.)*

Brad: And now, if you'll excuse me, I have a class to take. I believe its women's weightlifting in the west wing. *(Exit.)*

Tracey: What happened?

Richard: He tricked me.

Doris: And he stole *my* buckets to do it!

Tracey: How cruel! A trick Dick Quick nick.

Richard: I just thought I was helping him. *(There is banging and crashing from outside, then Brad shrieks. He staggers on, his hair tangled, his shirt ripped, and his shorts half off.)*

Brad: Help me! Help me!

Doris: What's the problem?

Brad: It's the women weightlifters. I was just showing them my perfectly-formed physique. They went berserk! They attacked me.

Doris: Don't be so silly. It's just a load of over-excited women. Get right back in there.

Brad: I'm not going back in there. Never! No way! They'll rip the clothes off me. They'll rip the limbs off me! *(To Richard.)* You've got to help me.

Richard: I think I'd better go and clean up. *(Exit.)*

Brad: *(To Tracey.)* Will you help me?

Tracey: After all you've done to me? *(Exit.)*

Brad: *(To Doris.)* Help me, please.

Doris: Something tells me you should have thought about that some time ago. *(Exit.)*

Brad: Whatever shall I do? There's no one left. Why on earth did I behave so badly to everyone? Now I'm alone just at the moment I need people most. *(Enter Mrs Judge.)*

Mrs Judge: Is it convenient to come in?

Brad: *(Coarsely.)* What do you want?

Mrs Judge: Oh I'm sorry. I never come in where I'm not invited. I'll leave. *(Exit.)*

Brad: No no! Please come back. *(Mrs Judge returns.)* I don't know what's wrong with me. Don't go. Anyone's company would be good.

Mrs Judge: You seem to be in some distress!

Brad: Ah! I've done some wrong things. And now all the consequences are rebounding on me.

Mrs Judge: I see! And do you wish you hadn't done these things?

Brad: Of course I'm glad I did them. Those stupid little people! ... *(Sobs.)* I ... I ... I ... I wish I hadn't done them. They've left me all alone, and they're the only friends I've got. Oh this is stupid. I've never cried in my entire life.

Mrs Judge: Have you thought of saying sorry?

Brad: Sorry?

Mrs Judge: Yes! It's not a popular word. You can never undo the wrong things you've done. Once you've done them they have happened and you can't 'unhappen' them. But you can be forgiven! And if you are truly sorry and truly forgiven, it's as if the wrong things never happened.

Brad: You're right! Of course, you're right! I shall say sorry. I shall ask everyone to forgive me, first thing in the morning.

Mrs Judge: That's my man! And now I believe you have a class to take.

Brad: I have! And I can face it now. Knowing this I can face anything. Thank you so much. All right wayward women, here I come! *(He goes. There is a clattering and banging outside and a scream. His shirt is flung on stage. Mrs Judge catches it.)*

Mrs Judge: I think I'm needed! Hold on there. I'm coming to help. *(Exit.)*

EPISODE 4

Tracey: *(Answering phone.)* Bodybuilders Health Club. Can I help you? Yes, yes ... no, no. *(Sympathetically.)* ... yes, yes ... Try putting your big toe in your navel and stretching your neck ... Triffic ... Goodbye. *(Enter Doris.)* Good morning Doris.

Doris: Haven't got time for good mornings today Tracey. We've got one more day to get this place cleared up before the inspector comes and we've barely started yet. Ah! Dust on the floor again! Could you pass me that dustpan and brush please. *(Tracey brings it out and Doris begins to sweep, down on her knees. As she does so, Richard enters and stands the other side of Doris from Tracey.)*

Tracey: Good morning Richard.

Richard: Good morning Tracey.

Both: Aaaah! *(They shut their eyes and go to kiss each other. As they do so Doris gets up between them, so they actually kiss her on both cheeks.)*

Doris: Come on! No time for that! There's floors to be swept before you can even think about yucky stuff.

Richard: Right! Give me the brush Doris. I'll do it in no time. The floor will be brushed in one slick Dick Quick flick. *(He starts to brush.)*

Tracey: We'd better start dusting the gym equipment. *(They do. As they are dusting, Brad enters. Tracey and Doris see him and hide in alarm behind a vaulting horse or similar piece of gym equipment. Richard goes on brushing unawares, until he realizes he is brushing Brad's feet. He slowly looks up, shrieks and runs to hide behind the horse, pushing Doris out one end as he does so. Doris yelps, runs round and dives in the other side, pushing Tracey out. Tracey does the same, pushing Richard out. Richard does the same, pushing Doris out. Doris is about to repeat this when ...)*

Brad: Stop! Come out you two. *(They emerge, hiding behind Doris.)* I've got something to say. This is hard for me. Doris, I've been horrid to you and called you names. I'm sorry. Tracey, I've shouted at you for something that wasn't your fault. I'm sorry. Richard, I took advantage of you just because you're puny. I'm sorry. I've learnt my lesson.

Richard: Brad, this is not like your usual self. What's come over you?

Brad: Well, there was a stranger walked in here yesterday and, talking to her, I realised I need to be forgiven.

Richard and Tracy: *(Together.)* Oh! You've seen her too! *(To each other.)* Oh! Does this mean you've seen her as well? *(To Brad.)* I thought I was the only one.

Doris: Hang on. What do you mean?

Richard and Tracey: *(Together.)* The one who comes in here every day. I thought the others were making it up.

Doris: Well, I don't know anything about that. And I don't know what Mrs Judge from the council will say about our security if she finds we've got strange women wandering in.

Brad: Mrs Judge! Hey, isn't it tomorrow that she comes?

Doris: It is, and if those windows aren't clean it's not even worth her looking in.

Brad: Right. Get sponging. And just to show I've changed, I'll lead the way. *(They line up, take wet sponges from a bucket in this order – Brad, Tracey, Richard, Doris. They start sponging an imaginary window in front of them. Then Tracey and Richard catch each others' eyes, sigh and gaze at each other. As they do so, the sponging hands go wider adrift until they are sponging Doris' and Brad's faces instead.)* Um! Excuse me, but would you be so kind as to refrain from doing that.

Doris: Good grief. He has changed!

Tracey: So sorry!

Brad: Goodness! Is that the time? I've got to go and take vicar's volleyball on the veranda. See you! *(Exit.)*

Tracey: My word! I've to to take pregnant paddlers in the pool. I'll be back. *(Exit.)*

Richard: And I've got to take weaklings' work-out in the weights room. Tracey, wait for me! *(Exit.)*

Doris: What! You can't leave me to do it all by myself. I can't manage ... Please ... Won't you ... Oh no! *(She sits down, depressed. Enter Mrs Judge.)*

Mrs Judge: Excuse me.

Doris: Who are you?

Mrs Judge: Oh, no one special. I've just been popping over the last few days to see if I can help.

Doris: So they were right. There has been a strange woman in here last week.

Mrs Judge: Not strange! Just a stranger! But it does seem that I have arrived just when I was needed, so perhaps it's a good job I was here. You don't look very happy.

Doris: Well, the whole health club has got to be cleaned before the inspector comes tomorrow. I'm all by myself. I'll never manage it. I'm not strong enough.

Mrs Judge: My dear lady, why don't you ask for help?

Doris: There's no one here to ask. *(Mrs Judge does a self–effacing cough.)* You! Oh I couldn't possibly ask you!

Mrs Judge: Nothing could give me greater pleasure than to help you clean, decorate and make the whole place new. All I'm waiting for is...

Doris: Yes?

Mrs Judge: To be asked!

Doris: Oh, please would you. Please, please, please.

Mrs Judge: *(Rolling sleeves.)* Just show me where you want to begin.

Doris: Right here. *(Gives her sponge.)*

Mrs Judge: Let's try cleaning my way. You'll find it's more fun that you ever imagined. *(There is music, something like the hokey-cokey, and they clean rhythmically, do a few dance steps, clean, and dance off scrubbing as they go.)*

EPISODE 5

(The room is much, much tidier than before. There is no one on stage. The phone rings. No one to reply! Doris rushes on and answers it.)

Doris: Bodybuilders Health Club. Can I help you? ... She's not here ... I can't help it if she's always here, she's not here at the moment ... Yes, no, yes, no, yes, no ... I haven't the faintest idea. *(She yells.)* Tracey! *(Tracey comes.)* There's a man here with his leg stuck round his neck, his arm stuck under his ankle and his nose stuck up his belly button. Can you help him?

Tracey: *(Takes the phone.)* Bodybuilders Health Club. Can I h... There's no need to be like that ... Quite honestly I don't think you need a health club. If you really want to lose weight I suggest you become a Sumo wrestler. Good day! *(She puts the phone down. Brad enters.)* Good morning Brad.

Brad: Good morning T... good grief. Is this the same health club that I've been coming to these last five days. It's transformed! It's spotless! It's beautiful!

Doris: It's Richard! *(Enter Richard.)*

Tracey: Good morning Richard.

Richard: This is wonderful! Bodybuilders Health Club has never had such a great hour. I shall never call you just Doris again. You have become Doris the Dazzling! The cleaner with class!

Doris: Don't take the mick Dick Quick. Yick! Besides I could never have done it myself. I owe this entirely to the help of the woman who came to visit us yesterday. I don't suppose we shall ever see her again, but she has completely changed our prospects.

All: Agreed! *(The phone rings.)*

Tracey: Oh no, not again. Excuse me! *(She picks up the phone.)* Look, I don't care if you are stuck in a knot. You'll just have to get a job as a contortionist ... *(Her face drops.)* Oh! Mrs Judge! Yes, we're expecting you.

From the council! Any minute now. Yes, we'll be ready. Triffic! Bye! *(She puts the phone down.)* The moment's arrived. She's coming any minute now.

Doris: Don't worry. We're ready for her. In a line everyone. *(They do.)* Stand to attention. *(They do.)* Broad smile. *(They do.)* Introducing the inspector, Mrs Judge. *(Enter Mrs Judge.)*

All: You!!!

Mrs Judge: Good morning everybody. I see you were expecting me.

Brad: Well, we weren't expecting you, we were expecting ... you!

Mrs Judge: Then I'm glad you're so pleased to see me. And I must say what a splendid place you have here. It is perfectly decorated and beautifully clean.

Doris: Yes, but only because you made it like that.

Mrs Judge: And what splendid people on the staff. Richard, for example, not in the least worried that he's not so strong and not so good looking; just happy that he's loving and a well-loved person.

Richard: Yes, but only because you made me like that.

Mrs Judge: And Tracey. You've found someone to listen to you and someone you're prepared to listen to. What valuable things you have learnt!

Tracey: Yes, but only because you made me like that.

Mrs Judge: And Brad. Not a perfectly good person, but a forgiven person; ready to say sorry, to be sorry, and to make a new start.

Brad: Yes, but only because you made me like that.

Mrs Judge: Well, I have no hesitation in giving this club its new license. As far as I'm concerned, I would be delighted if you stay in business forever.

All: Yes, but only because you made us like that. *(The phone rings.)*

Mrs Judge: Excuse me! *(She picks up the phone.)* Bodybuilders Health Club. Can I help you? Oh I'm so sorry! Well, first try relaxing ... Good ... Now try straightening up ... Good ... Now try standing up ... Marvellous ... Oh I'm so pleased, and I hope it changes your life forever ... Some advice! Well yes! I suggest you join a health club and I think I know exactly which one you would enjoy ... The people? Well, they aren't perfect! Some of the time they are not even good! But they have got their heart in the right place, and even if they do let me down, I'm not going to let them down ... Well, straight away ... we'll be waiting for you. Why not come j–j–j–j–jiving down the gym?!

All: Shake that body!

Extra time craft activities

A selection of craft activities loosely based around the theme of bodies.

FOR BLUE BELTS (aged 5–7)

WAX CRAYON RUBBINGS

MOBILES

HATS

WEAVING

MARZIPAN SWEETS

PERCUSSION INSTRUMENTS – FROM PAPER CUPS WITH LENTILS INSIDE

EGG SHELL PICTURES

PAPER PLATE MASKS

LIFE-SIZE PORTRAITS DRAWN ON LINING PAPER ROUND A FRIEND

FINGER PUPPETS – FROM FELT AND STRING

FINGER PRINTING

FOR BLACK BELTS (aged 8–11)

PIPE CLEANER MODELS

UNKNOCKDOWNABLE CLOWN –
FROM HALF A PING-PONG BALL
STUFFED WITH PLASTICINE

KITES

MASKS – FROM A
LARGE BROWN PAPER
BAG, WITH PAPER CONES
AND PIPE CLEANERS

BRACELETS

POP-UP CARDS

Something for a rainy day!

GINGERBREAD
PEOPLE

STRING PRINTING

FACE PAINTING

PAPER-BAG PUPPETS